W9-BKD-671

Printed in the United States of America

First Printing, May 2018

ISBN 978-1732238909

KITCat Publishing
For information contact kitcatpublishing@gmail.com

Cover Design by Design_Palace/Fiverr.com
Cover Photo ©Aivolie/Shutterstock.com
Photo of Simba by Elliott Tessler
Other photos, unless identified in the caption, provided by the Knopman
Family

For my family and friends, human and furry ones, who bring light, love and laughter into my life every day.

Measure Your Cat's IQ

Tales from the Devilish Genius to the Feeble Minded Fuzz Ball

By Calla H. Knopman

"Clearly, animals know more than we think, and think a great deal more than we know."

Irene M. Pepperberg

Table of Contents

"Intelligence in the cat is underrated. "

Louis Wain

Introduction

The domestic house cat may be the most intelligent creature on the planet. You can stop laughing now, it's true! They manage to manipulate other animals, and us naive humans, to get what they want and yet still wiggle deeper into our hearts simply by purring like a motorboat or snuggling into our sides at night. Out of the estimated 74 Million cats in the United States, you might have a Kitty Einstein living with you but how can you know? The conundrum is; how can we state how smart a cat is without a way to measure or qualify the Kitty IQ? This is exactly what *Measure Your Cat's IQ* is going to address.

In *Measure Your Cat's IQ* you will find:

- ✓ A breakdown of categories that will quantify kitty intelligence over various aspects of behavior and thought patterns.
- ✓ Test and experiments you and your family can do with your feline.
- ✓ A rating system to quantify the tests.
- ✓ Examples of other cats' scores to follow along with throughout the book.
- ✓ Tales of adventures and mayhem of kitties for each category.

In addition, the provided template for the Kitty Communication Journal will assist you in increasing the communication patterns with your kitty for a more satisfying relationship.

Each chapter of the book will be broken down into a short academic introduction of the category followed by one or more sections. Each section will describe the behavior or intellectual area we will be scoring followed by a test. Tales are included to provide example responses ranging from those Devilish Genius kitties all the way down to the Feeble Minded Fuzz Ball.

The last section of the book contains the information to collect and total all your kitty's scores to determine the IQ level.

Have fun and be sure to post your own stories, your cat's IQ measurement and browse our templates and other readers' postings on our Facebook page at www.facebook.com/measureyourcatsiq .

Kitty IQ Scale:

When we consider Kitty IQ and how to measure it, we need to recognize that we can't rate our furry brethren on the same scale as we would a human. After all, we can't make the cats take a written test, tell us what the first response is to a Rorschach ink blot or measure their mental age. Instead, we need to develop a scale based on observed kitty behaviors against potential reactions both positive and negative.

To quantify this, I developed a system that rates a cat within five levels of IQ, the middle being the average with two incremental levels above and two below. The categories are: Devilish Genius, Psycho Superior, Average Kitty, Borderline Baby and bringing up the rear, Feeble Minded Fuzz Ball.

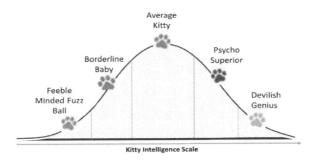

Figure 1- IQ Bell Curve

Below is a description of each level of Kitty IQ along with an example of what a kitty response would be for that rating. For instance, when you set down the plate of food, the different levels of kitties respond as follows:

🐾 **The Devilish Genius** can have total disdain for those things we are so proud to be able to offer to the loved fur ball. The disdain is shown with a look at the bowl and then you. Kitty is communicating that this is not food.

Figure 2- Devilish Genius Response ©Fantam_rd/Shutterstock.com

He didn't say that he didn't like the smell, taste or texture. That would be too normal. The Devilish Genius will make you question if it actually **IS** food. You may wonder where you put the receipt so you can take the rest of the case back to the pet store.

The Devilish Genius kitty is very independent and at times will do those amazing cat antics that seem beyond belief. A good example is our Somali male, Alex, who learned from watching the kids, that a 'Time-Out' for bad behavior meant he had to go sit facing the corner until told the time-out period was over. It sounds fantastic but we will cover this adventure in the *Analytical Thinking* chapter.

The Psycho Superior uses a slightly less brilliant method to control his or her environment. In this case, the kitty is attempting to let you know that although the bowl does contain food, it was not the type expected or asked for. As if this is a restaurant!

Figure 3 - Psycho Superior Response ©Fantam_rd/Shutterstock.com

The Psycho Superior kitty works within the boundaries of our world but twists reality in order to support his unique requirements. This kitty is amused by us and can often be seen smirking. A perfect example is an all-black male cat I had once called Houdini, who tortured the dog by running under the couch, and out the other end without the dog knowing. Houdini then sat on the arm of the couch above him looking superior while the dog was busy barking at the entry point. If the dog bothered to look up, Houdini would be in serious trouble. You have to know your audience... which this kitty did.

The Average Kitty exhibits normal behavior that we expect from kitty. No flashes of brilliance but no bouncing off the walls either. This is a fun kitty to have. He generally eats his food without a lot of fuss or fanfare.

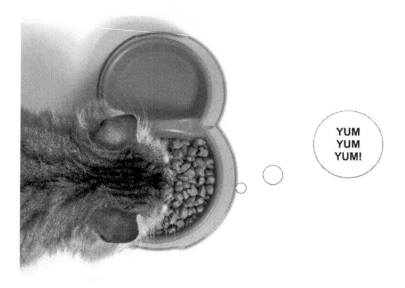

Figure 4- Average Kitty Response ©Fantam_rd/Shutterstock.com

He probably does not wake you up in the middle of the night climbing up the bookcase or pushing books off of the headboard to fall on you. Overall, Average Kitty is a happy fellow, who enjoys sleeping, playing, eating and being a companion to the family.

The Borderline Baby, on the other hand, may actually bounce off of wall. He is a little less sure of his place in the overall household and questions how he fits in. He doesn't take anything for granted and generally appreciates what he is given.

Figure 5- Borderline Baby Response - ©Fantam_rd/SHutterstock.com

He can come off as a needy cat because he recognizes his dependence on the human family and may be constantly underfoot in his attempt to stick close to his human parent. At times Borderline Baby kitty seems to be missing neurons or having them fire indiscriminately. A prime example is the cat, not kitten but full grown adult cat, who is chasing her tail because she is not sure it is hers. We expect this behavior from kittens, which would be normal but in an adult cat, this a bit less than brilliant and is definitely borderline behavior.

The Feeble Minded Fuzz Ball make us wonder, if perhaps he was shaken a bit or dropped when a little tyke. He may stare at objects for what seems to be a very long time before initiating an action.

Figure 6-Feeble Minded Fuzz Ball Response - ©Fantam_rd/Shutterstock.com

Patience is an absolute must to be a loving custodian to a FM kitty. But it is totally worth it. These guys are just so cute you can't help but love them but some of the antics are so far out of normal that it makes you shake your head. A good example of this is Nicky who can't follow a toy or laser if it is moving at standard speeds. To play with Nicky you have to move the toy very slowly so he can track the movements. If you go fast in any direction he will leave the playing field and go sit down to take a nap.

IQ Rating by Category

Of course, cats have a wide variety of responses to different stimuli. A cat who appears to be a genius in one aspect of life can be completely feeble minded in another. Take the cat that is so aware of his family and external dangers that he puts his own life at risk to chase away an aggressive dog[1].

---

[1] *https://www.youtube.com/watch?v=ftIRIPcsqxo*

Measure Your Cat's IQ

The same kitty can run racing from the room when you sneeze. Is he Super Kitty or Scaredy cat? Actually, he is both. This shouldn't be a surprise. We humans also have our moments of brilliance and moments somewhat less so. For instance, I can tune a client's workflow to reduce processing time often by 90% but I simply cannot figure out how decorative pillows should be displayed on a bed!

The remainder of *Measure Your Cat's IQ* is broken into chapters, each focused on a different aspect of kitty life and behavior that can be rated for cognitive development kitty IQ. Each group of stories will be followed by an example rating with a space to record your own kitty's measurement as well. Additional templates can be found in the appendix or on www.facebook.com/MeasureYourCatsIQ.

Use the scale shown in the table below to add or subtract points from your cat's IQ rating as we go. Some categories and tests will add points to your kitty score, some will only subtract points and some will provide the opportunity to add or subtract to your cat's IQ score.

Category	Points
Devilish Genius	Add 5 points
Psycho Superior	Add 3 points
Average Kitty	0 Points
Borderline Baby	Subtract 3 points
Feeble Minded Fuzz Ball	Subtract 5 point

We will use two cats throughout the book in our example ratings, Gabby and Nicky. Gabby is an 8 year old female Ocicat, which is a mix of Abyssinian and Siamese breeds. The Ocicat is known for its intelligence, energy and devotion to the family. A picture of our Gabby as a kitten is below. Note the adorable spots.

Figure 7- Kitten Gabby Sleeping on a Pillow

Nicky is a 7 year old male Somali. Somalis are long haired Abyssinians known as the 'Fox Cat' due to their appearance. They are celebrated for their playfulness, love of water and attachment to family. A picture of Nicky is below where he is emulating me at work. He mirrored my position with the computer on my lap and feet up on the desk.

Figure 8- Nicky at Work

While reading through the book and taking the test, feel free to navigate the chapters in whatever order you prefer. There will however, be references between chapters as stories may touch on subjects across sections. The final chapter will walk through calculating the overall score and its meaning.

The first category we will cover is *Analytical Thinking* and kitty cognitive development.

"I've met many thinkers and many cats, but the wisdom of cats is infinitely superior."

Hippolyte Taine

Chapter 1: Cats – analytical beings?

I first started thinking about kitty cognitive capabilities when I was a psychology major interested in adolescent development as a focus. I would learn about development theories including Piaget's and test these out on my cats and neighbor's children. My cat's scored better. Yes, there are ways we can test Piaget's theory of cognitive development with our cats. Let's take a closer look while converting the tests into those we can utilize with a kitty.

The first stage called, "sensorimotor" tests the subject's ability to understand object permanence. In kitty parlance this is simply what I call the 'Out of sight out of mind' test. Show the kitty a toy and keep their attention by playing with it. Then hide the toy behind your back or someplace out of site and see if your cat finds it.

Kittens and young children would have no idea what happened to their toy but most adult cats will immediately go behind your back to retrieve the toy wondering what is wrong with **you**. Aha, Kitty is has passed the first stage.

Rating Opportunity: This test will only subtract points from your kitty's score if deserved.

This is the object permanence test. Initiate kitty play with a toy that can be held in your hand. After a couple of minutes, hide the toy behind your back. What does kitty do?

- ☙ If kitty is older than 6 months and cannot find the toy, then subtract 3 points from kitty's score.
- ☙ If kitty finds the toy, add no points, this is expected behavior.

Cat's Name	Category	Rating	Short Reason
Gabby	Analytical Thinking: Out of sight test	0	Gabby has mastered the object permanence
Nicky	Analytical Thinking: Out of sight test	0	Nicky also finds the object immediately

The second level is called the "preoperational" stage. This is where subjects learn to understand images and symbols, and begin to play act or make pretend. I can tell you emphatically that cats may achieve this stage. For instance, there is a YouTube video available in which a man taught his cat to play dead when he 'pretends' to shoot him with his finger. I cracked up laughing at this. Do your own search for this to watch and enjoy. Do we all agree that this proves the point? My own kitties have in the past pretended to be hurt in order to get the treat they were asking for. This is the famous; "hold up paw and look sad" meant to melt your heart and give kitty comfort.

Rating Opportunity: This test will only add points from your kitty's score if deserved. This is a more difficult aspect to test with kitties. The classic test with children is to engage them in play to gauge understanding of language and initiate play acting. We cannot test this with kitties however we can test the other characteristics that accompany this stage. For instance, playing pretend or demonstrating an understanding of symbols.

Think of some animals you have seen in movies. They are trained to act a part or role. For instance making pretend their paw is hurt or playing dead. Does your kitty show this aspect of pretending? Does it understand symbols?

🐾 If your kitty is capable of playing pretend or understanding symbols, then add 3 points to kitty's score.

Cat's Name	Category	Rating	Short Reason
Gabby	Analytical Thinking: Pretend	+3	Gabby makes pretend her eye or paw hurt to get attention. She also picks her food by color and container (bag, can, etc...).
Nicky	Analytical Thinking: Pretend	+3	Nicky is a master of playing pretend. From faking a pain somewhere to pretending to be asleep. He even pretend snores (he really does snore)

If you thought the second level was difficult, you are going to love the third. The third stage, "Concrete Operational" is concerned with the concept of conservation and mathematics. The third level's classic psychological test is the water test. In the water test the same volume of water is poured into different sized glasses. Usually one is wide and the other tall. A subject who passes this test must recognize that despite the glass shape, it is the same volume of water. We obviously cannot use this test for kitty. However, the third stage is also marked by logical reasoning. Ah-ha, here is something we can reasonably look for signs of in kitty. For instance, Nicky stares at some artwork (paintings) for extended periods of time. He is particularly drawn to ones that show water. I put a bar stool underneath his favorite picture, which is a beach scene with waves crashing and the sun setting on the horizon. I was interested to see what he would do and I have to tell you, I was astounded. He put his paw up on the painting and was feeling the waves to see if they were moving.

Rating Opportunity:

I believe there is some evidence that cats can achieve level 3. If you have observed behavior that has convinced you this is true, then take the next test but be prepared to justify your answer.

🐾 If you think your kitty has reached this stage, give 5 points. This stage constitutes the use of inductive logic and reasoning as well as the initial understanding of empathy.

Cat's Name	Category	Rating	Short Reason
Gabby	Analytical Thinking: Cognitive Development	0	No indication as of yet
Nicky	Analytical Thinking: Cognitive Development	+5	Nicky stares at pictures for hours. One in particular with the ocean and waves he continues to try to touch and see if it is moving. Very unusual.

Stage 4 is the formal operations stage is when cognitive development reaches the ability to abstract concepts such as math and science. I am going to skip this, perhaps the next book ☺

I am sure the first section of this chapter was a surprise to many. I have often heard folks say that cats are not capable of analytical thought and that their actions are based purely on instinct. My response to this is, "Balderdash!" Here are some more examples you may have seen in your kitty as well.

Houdini Teaches Me Who is Boss

We had an all-black male cat named Houdini. Houdini was perhaps the funniest cat I have ever had. He loved to play tricks on me such as disappearing and reappearing at will. I named him Houdini because his was the son of my cat Magic, an all-black female. I thought it was a fitting name and he certainly lived up to it.

At the time, in our house, a spray bottle full of tap water was used as a standard tool to teach kitty what constituted unacceptable behavior. Just as with children, you can't say, "No" to everything. You need to pick the top three or four things which are critical to either kitty's health or to protect the human family members.

One of the critical things to manage was Houdini destroying my college text books. As I was studying, he wanted nothing more than to get between me and the book and if he found a text book when I wasn't paying attention, it was shredded in minutes. Spritz, Spritz, Spritz! And have you met a kitty who deserved it more?

One day I came home to a mini flood in my room. It took me a bit to reconstruct what had happened. There was water everywhere with bits of notebook scattered, both the pages and plastic cover reduced to shreds. After careful examination, I could see distributed randomly in this mess were tiny pieces of clear plastic. I looked around and could not find the spray bottle anywhere.

Yes, the little monster had reduced the spray bottle along with my notebooks (including Piaget's theorem) to taters. I think Piaget would likely rate this act firmly in the third stage of cognitive development!

Now, this was not a random act on his part. It took thought, planning and execution...not to mention that he had to time it correctly. After all, if I came in too early, it could have ruined the surprise.

So, there sat Houdini, on the top of the bookcase, out of reach, watching my reaction to see what would happen.

I grabbed a beer, walked into the den, lit a smoke and turned the TV on. After all, the cat had won. There was no response to his activity that made any sense. Houdini sashayed past the den on his way outdoors with a smug little expression on his kitty face. The little bastard!

I eventually cleaned up the mess and never bought another spray bottle.

Lights On, Lights Off

Simba is a handsome cat adopted by Elliott, a good friend with lots of love to give to this lucky boy. Elliott drove a couple of states away to pick up Simba who was desperately searching for his forever home.

Figure 9-Simba Exploring

It was love at first sight and a perfect match for Simba who needed someone with patience to break through the wall he had built to protect himself. In the beginning, Simba was very skittish and didn't want to be touched or held but after time, patience and being exposed to Elliott's love and warmth, Simba is a new cat. One happy boy, he gets cuddled and protected as the precious kitty he is. Nice when a story ends well, isn't it?

As a matter of fact, Simba is so comfortable and full of confidence now that he can exercise his natural feline curiosity. He is actually pushing the envelope for kitty analytical thinking and, thus, gets included in this chapter.

One night Elliott was sleeping soundly in the bedroom and something unusual woke him up. There was a strange sound that didn't make sense so he initially thought there was an intruder in the house. Elliott got up to investigate and as soon as he approached the doorway he could see the lights turning off and on. What kind of robber would keep flipping the light switch?

Confused and concerned, Elliott stepped through the doorway and was shocked at the actual cause. There was Simba staring up at the light switch and jumping up the wall to turn it off, then on, then off, then on...Elliott was astounded. His little kitty was jumping more than five feet in the air to play with the light switch in the hallway. Lights on, lights off and no clapper. This explains the strange noises.

Let's break this down. Why would a cat turn on the lights? Even if a cat wanted to turn on lights, why choose the hallway? My supposition is that Simba's objective was to wake up his father. He could have done this action down stairs or in the basement and nobody would have been the wiser but he didn't. He chose the hallway right outside the bedroom.

Secondly, notice how Simba associated the hallway lights on with Elliott rising. Now it makes perfect sense. "I want my daddy up to play with me and he always turns on the hallway light when waking up, so let's give him a little nudge to get him started." I think this kitty deserves 5 points for analytical thinking.

Who Doesn't Belong Here: A Magic story

One day I was home enjoying a TV dinner in the den. Magic came running in the room, jumped up on the couch and started meowing at me. This was a different meow, not a single food meow while walking around my legs; this was a grouping of meows which I had never heard from her before. After her meows, she jumped down, ran to the door and then turned and meowed again at me. I smiled and said, just a minute and took another bite of food. Magic ran back, jumped on the couch next to me and started the meowing again and then ran to the door. I knew I would never get to eat in peace if I didn't see whatever it was she wanted to show me.

I followed her out of the den through the hallway. Magic stepped on Harry, the dog who was snoozing at the kitchen entrance. She ran over the length of Harry and to the kitchen door. Front paws went up on the door and Magic reached for the knob all the while meowing.

Figure 10- Magic Showing the Strangers at the Door - ©Chipmunk131/Shutterstock.com

I looked up and there were 3 guys with the screen door opened trying to jimmy the kitchen door. I looked at them; they looked me and started working faster. I turned around, kicked Harry awake and pointed at the door. Now, once Harry saw the men, he jumped into action, ran at the door with the big German Shepard bark 'WOOF, WOOF, WOOF!" which means, "Make my day dudes." The guys ran off and I called the police.

Magic proved that she could tell the difference between people who belong, proper ways to get invited in and who to escalate concerns to. I rate this as genius and worthy of 5 points. As you may have guessed, Magic ate the rest of my turkey dinner as a thank you and Harry did not.

Rating Opportunity: This category is only to add points to your kitty's score if deserved. What actions of your cats have you believing there is careful analysis and decision making going on in the kitty brain? Has kitty ever out thought you like Houdini did?

- 🐾 If so, please add the points 3 or 5 based on the brilliance of the method kitty used.
- 🐾 If you have not seen signs of this in your kitty yet, you may still over time. Come back and update their score.

In our tales in this chapter, I would give 5 points to Simba, Houdini and Magic.

Cat's Name	Category	Rating	Short Reason
Gabby	Analytical Thinking & Decision Making	+3	Gabby shows this in all aspects of our interaction. She looks at the hand doing the movement, not the toy. She unpacks my suitcase so I can't go on the road and more.
Nicky	Analytical Thinking & Decision Making	0	Nicky shows nothing of significance.

"If animals could speak, the dog would be a blundering outspoken fellow, but the cat would have the rare grace of never saying a word too much. "

Mark Twain

Chapter 2: Verbal Communication – The Art of the Meow

Cats have a wide range of verbal communication protocols at their command. There is the ordinary meow for food, one for play, the complaint meow for "Clean my pail" or even the meow directed to another cat, "Get off my spot!", and then we have the "Mommy look at me" meow. Cats also have a full range of hissing and growling vocalizations for fear, warning or promise of retribution. And let's not forget those funny mouth movements and the cute chatter when they see prey. Some cats can even chuff like a big cat or may squeak, like a Siamese.

How does your cat meow and can you use that to improve your conversation?

Human Cat Communication

Yes, I do talk to my cats. Sometimes I am not quite sure what I am saying but it is easier to try and imitate them than attempt to get them to imitate me. This does not stop my mom from endlessly repeating phrases like "Food" to the cats while they look at her like she is speaking Greek.

There are a number of cat 'words' that I can differentiate and imitate. For instance, the tone and length of a call for food is completely different from the follow up begging.

- ☙ "Meeh-owww" is the first call for food which stands for "It's time."
- ☙ "Mmm-uh" is the follow up meaning "Come on, let's go."
- ☙ "Mmm" is short for, "Oh, for Pete's Sake, this is one stupid human".

A kitty may vocalize in a way that doesn't resemble a meow at all, while others sound like strangled versions of a meow along the lines of 'uh-aow', 'urrr' or even 'errrr'.

Rating opportunity: The Meow Test.- Can you speak cat? How does your cat meow and what can you identify as the differentiator for various kitty requests? Follow along and note your cat's type, length and reason for meowing using our *Cat Communications Journal* template available on www.facebook.com/Measureyourcatsiq or in the appendix section at the end of this book.

Try and imitate your cat's vocalizations and get kitty to respond to you. If you have problems getting kitty to respond, you might need to start off with an eye blink which we will cover in a later section. It may take some time to properly imitate cat speak to a degree where they will understand and try to teach you how to speak kitty.

- ☙ If you can get a back and forth going for at least 5 responses, give your cat 5 points because kitty is attempting to teach you how to talk correctly.
- ☙ If the response ends after a time or two add 3 points. Kitty is frustrated that you just aren't smart enough.
- ☙ 0 points for no response, kitty thinks you are crazy or he simply can't understand your kitty talk.
- ☙ Subtract 3 points if your cat has no interest and walks away.
- ☙ Subtract 5 points if the cat gets angry.

Note* Make sure you are attempting to imitate curious sounds, not angry ones. Do not hiss at your cat!

Cat's Name	Category	Rating	Short Reason
Gabby	Verbal Communication: Human -Cat	+5	Gabby is a master at communication with humans. She gets her point across with meows and responds to my meows as well as English. I can get Gabby to understand my meows for toys and food. Still working on our kitty glossary ☺
Nicky	Verbal Communication: Human -Cat	+3	Nicky does respond back and forth with me and immediately responds to 'Food', 'Treat', 'Out', 'In' and some others. He follows directions well, such as 'don't eat Gabby's food' but does seem to have selective hearing!

Different Dialects of Kitty Talk

Do you think all cats speak a common kitty language and can understand each other? How about a cat from Rome and one from New York? Sounds silly doesn't it, but I think something similar is at work. As a matter of fact, Lund[2] University is funding a study to research if cats have an accent based on their geography. I'd really like to speak to these guys about thinking across breeds as well as regionally.

---

[2] http://www.newsweek.com/cats-accents-phonetics-lund-university-441779

Our latest family additions are two kitten adoptions, one Somali and one Ocicat. A Somali is a long haired Abyssinian and an Ocicat is a mix between an Abyssinian and Siamese.

We welcomed Gabby, the female Ocicat first and then Alex, the male Somali joined our family about a month later. From the very first it was apparent that not only did the two kittens have a different manner of speaking but they seemed to have trouble understanding each other.

Figure 11- Kitty Dialects Translation

Gabby squeaked along in her incredibly cute broken up kitten talk, "mia-ah-ow" while Alex did his straightforward "meaw" almost with a drawl like a Texan. The funniest part was that I kept catching one kitten cocking his head to the side listening to the other one. Over time, their meows have standardized as if they invented their own way to communicate with each other.

Evidence of Super Hearing

Even if your cat did not respond to you in the 'Meow Test', don't worry, he definitely heard you and is taking in the activity for future thought. Cats can hear sounds much better than we humans can; in fact, they can detect frequencies up to approximately 79 kHz. This is a greater range than humans or dogs which cap out at 20 kHz and 45 kHz, respectively. Let's look a little more closely at this super kitty hearing.

Who is waiting for you when you walk through the door? Is your husband or wife there with you slippers and martini? Are the children waiting to show you the new artwork of the day? Even if you do have the 'Leave it to Beaver' experience, how do they know of your imminent arrival?

If your house is like mine, family members are following the lead of the kitty. Cats are known to be aware of their owner's arrival long before the car approaches the driveway, assuming that the cat actually cares or has an investment in monitoring the family member that is.

The family cat can not only identify the difference in your car from your neighbors but can detect it minutes before family members can even see it. My family tells me that the cats run downstairs a couple of minutes before I even turn onto the street. I drive a Mustang so perhaps they enjoy the purr of the engine, I know I do.

Due to kitty super hearing they are great predators, particularly in a city environment where construction always makes rodents run to find new homes. Years ago we lived in a ground floor apartment in Chicago right on Lake Michigan. The complex had a pier that extended into the lake and was a great place for fishing and a magnet for rodents. We had three cats at the time, PM, Falcor and Tokar who all loved that apartment. When the weather would turn cold, the mice would look for ways to get into a warmer abode. Got to love that lake effect snow!

One of the cats would hear something suspicious, focus on a spot, and the other two would come over to investigate. If there were three cats sitting around in a circle staring at the floor, I knew a critter was there trying to find a way in. I'd hunker down next to them and wait. In a few minutes, even I could hear the 'scratch-scratch-scratch' of little mice claws looking for a break in the flooring.

At this point the cats were in the attack mode, heads down on the floor by the paws, with butts up in the air waving side to side and tails flying. They would do this in complete silence, as the object of the game is to let the little rodent in and then 'play' with it. My objective however is to keep the little rodent OUT! I would get closer to the floor and issue a plaintive 'Meow' a couple of times. The scratching immediately stopped and all three cats turned to look at me in disgust. I apparently ruined a sure thing. We will talk more about playing with prey in a later chapter of the book.

Did you hear that? Silent communication

Have you ever seen your cats appearing to converse but you couldn't hear anything? Did you think they were using ESP? They may have been communicating at frequencies that our limited human hearing cannot detect. One way for us to catch this silent communication in action is observing a mother cat interact with her kittens.

PM was all gray, blue in the sunlight, with a petite, sleek body, long tail and the largest ears ever seen on such a little kitty. She had the appearance of subtle striping which disappeared as she aged. We adopted her when she was about the age of 8 weeks of age.

Figure 12- PM is Doing Her Job, Looking Cute

When PM was around 4 years old, I met my second husband, who had a male, all white, long haired cat named Tokar. We got married and they had kittens.

PM had six kittens, mostly white as they took after the proud papa. When it was time to nurse PM would lie down in the middle of the living room and within a few moments, all the kittens would come running from wherever they were and begin to nurse.

The first time I saw this silent communication in action, I thought perhaps I had missed hearing the call or the music was too loud. In the days following, I reduced the external noises to pay closer attention and sure enough PM's throat moved similar to a meow, but she emitted no sounds. I also observed times when a kitten or two would go to an area that was off limits, a throat move and ta-da, the kittens would come running back. Now bear in mind that the "off limits" was PM's setting not mine. She had no problems with them running amok in my underwear drawer and even used to open it for them. We'll cover *Boundaries* in a later chapter.

Rating Opportunity- Have you noticed any evidence of super hearing by your cat? Can he tell when the car is coming up the street? Does he tell you about strange people or animals that are around?

- Give your kitty 5 points if he has ever astounded you with super kitty hearing or detective skills.
- Give kitty 3 points if he is always waiting at the door for your arrival.
- Subtract 3 points if kitty seems more content to sun himself than greet you at the door, but he does look over to say hello when you get to the sun room he is in.
- Subtract 5 points if kitty is just not incented and is usually found lounging in the bed.

Cat's Name	Category	Rating	Short Reason
Gabby	Verbal Communication: Super Hearing	+5	Gabby has exceptional hearing. She tells me when the squirrels are digging in the flower garden... from upstairs!
Nicky	Verbal Communication: Super Hearing	+3	Nicky is always waiting at the door and tells me before the doorbell rings. He also seems to have phantom hearing that nobody else including Gabby believes.

Singing to Your Cat

Before we leave the acute audio capabilities of felines, it is worth noting their sensitivity and reactions to music. We all have heard that music soothes the savage beast and it is certainly true. You may ask, "What does musicality have to do with measuring intelligence? " I believe this is another form of communication such as the dog wailing away with my mom when she sings and plays the piano. The pet is showing interest in our activities and attempting to join in. While I have never heard of a cat meowing to a piano tune, I am sure it is possible. I have had kitties who do like the piano and catch them periodically playing with the keys. Now if kitty could find a way to use the pedals…. Well that would be another story. The objective here is that music does initiate a reaction from our pets and can be used to measure how they interact with environmental triggers.

We had a truly psychotic kitty, named Kelly, which was foisted on us from a friend who could not handle her. She was a rescue from the SPCA and we are not sure what her early kitten-hood was like but by the time we got Kelly, she hated everyone. And I mean **everyone**. Even those who fed her were on the list of humans she hated to deal with. She would hiss and attack constantly and none of our friends wanted to spend time in whatever room she was in.

We were at our wit's end when my brother happened onto an interesting phenomenon. Whenever he whistled 'My Cheri Amour' Kelly would come running from wherever she was, purring and wanting to get cuddled. Whistling that song would turn Kelly into a real social and likable kitty. Quit whistling, and she would revert back to hissing. Start whistling and she would go back to purring and head butting for attention…it was uncanny. Unfortunately, no one can whistle forever.

Gabby, who is normally a very happy cat, also responds both positively and negatively to music. When I sing Pearl Jam's 'In Hiding' she comes to the arm of my chair and begins to head butt my shoulder for cuddling. However, when I sing Anna Nalick's 'Breathe' the low notes make her paw at my mouth. This I assume, is to get me to stop singing either because I suck or because that particular note is like finger nails on a chalkboard to her. Since Gabby has all her claws, I tend to sing this song in lower volumes as I like my face without scratches.

Rating Opportunity: The singing test. Now it's time to experiment with your kitty. Have you noticed any reaction to music? If not, try and sing or whistle to your cat. Can you get a positive or negative response to musical stimuli? Try the old meow mix commercial if you recall it. You can also try making calls of other animals; a wolf howl or a bird chirp…. Remember, this is an experiment, not torture. If you find something the cat does not like, discontinue the stimulation.

- Give 5 points if you can elicit a strong positive reaction such as a head-butt or rolling on the floor.
- Add 3 points for a weak positive reaction such as the kitty sitting down to hear more tunes or staring at you while tilting head from side to side.
- Subtract 3 points for a weak negative reaction which would be kitty walking out of the room.
- Subtract 5 points if the kitty attacks you.

Cat's Name	Category	Rating	Short Reason
Gabby	Verbal Communication: Singing	+5	Gabby loves the high notes and cuddles. Hates the low notes
Nicky	Verbal Communication: Singing	-3	Nicky has no interest and walks away, disgusted

"If a cat does something, we call it instinct; if we do the same thing, for the same reason, we call it intelligence. "

Will Cuppy

Chapter 3: Non-Verbal Communication:

As much as I enjoy chatting with my kitties, they often tell just as much, if not more, with non-verbal communications. Just look at a cat for a couple of minutes and see what forms of communication it is sharing with you. Is the cat blinking, staring, twitching the tail, the ears, looking down or did kitty just lie down on the floor to show you its stomach? Each one of these actions is specific to a statement kitty is making to you.

Kitty can also speak volumes with his body, such as the head-butt, the body rub, touching parts of your arm or leg, and of course the ever popular figure eight between your legs while you are balancing food or trying to walk down the stairs. Sometimes I swear my cat is trying to kill me but then who would feed the little monster? By the way, 'Monster' is a term of endearment.

Now, kitties have to be exceptionally bright to communicate with us mentally handicapped humans who can't even speak Cat. Many of them have learned to say much without the need of a meow. Frankie, a rescue kitty, had a way of tilting her head to the side or pulling one ear half-way down that just said it all, "Are you serious?" Butterscotch, a calico female who was Magic's mother, would hold up a paw in the air as if to say,

"Don't make me get up. Talk to the paw". I learned to read kitty commentary and warnings pretty quickly as a kid.

Let's explore some of the non-verbal communication skills your kitty may be employing to speak with you.

Winkin', Blinkin' & Nod

A wink of an ear, a blink of an eye, a subtle nod, and cats can tell entire stories with their heads. The eyes, ears, nose and mouth can all give clear indications of kitty desire or warning. Some of these tells we can use to try and interpret what kitty is asking for and others should be clear signs when to pull back your hand.

An ear can go straight up, or down, may be cocked to the side, twitch back and forth, lie flat on the head or move to follow sound. The feline ear is more significant that just being a very soft place to pet. What are feline ears telling us with all these movements?

Ears twitching from side to side or up and back indicate that kitty is listening for some audio feed. I love watching cats move their ears to zero in on some sound that catches their attention. They look like little radar panels moving around while the rest of the head stays at attention. When they finally identify the source of the sound, they may well lose interest. The funny thing is that I started to notice that I do the same thing. If I hear a siren or noise coming from outside, I don't usually run to the window right away but move my head to attempt to locate the source of the noise. Now, I have to move my whole head but how cool would it be if I could just move my ears instead?

Ears can also be the first indicator of kitty stress and fear. When the ears start to fold back, watch out! The full blown fear response is unique to each cat but there are some commonalities. Let's start with the one that most humans find too cute in kittens and can't help but giggle at. The kitty puff!

A kitten, in an attempt to look large and more intimidating will puff up the tail, arch his back and face the object of his fear sideways.

Figure 13-Kitten Trying to Look Threatening - ©crazyfunnystuffCFS/YouTube.com

This actually makes the kitten appear two or three times its normal size. Cats are not the only animals that puff-up to appear larger than they are to dissuade potential predators. Certain species of frogs, porcupines and even gorillas do the puff. Cats, however, are the cutest in my opinion. This must be true for countless others too, as there are literally thousands of pictures and videos of cats in full puff mode posted on line. Because the objective of this book is to measure IQ, let's look a little more closely at the reasons and actions associated with the kitty puff.

A kitten approaches a mirror and sees in the reflection another cat looking at him. He makes some friendly gestures but the responses from the 'other' cat are confusing. He goes in closer to get a sniff and hits his nose on something. Ow! A simple swat at the mirror results in pain which elevates the threat. The kitten begins to fluff its tail to indicate its increased anxiety and guess what; the other cat does the same. The kitten now goes into full intimidation mode and arches its back. Oh my goodness, the other kitten in the mirror does the same. This must a bad dream! The kitty faces the mirror sideways and jumps closer to force the other cat to leave.

36

This can go on for a bit, moving along the sides of the mirror. Try to keep your laughter under control; even kittens do not like to be laughed at. Fortunately, kittens have very short attention spans and move on to the next curiosity very quickly.

Rating Opportunity: The Mirror Test: See how responsive your kitty is to visual stimuli. What does kitty do when you put a mirror on the floor for kitty to see himself? I used the type of mirror you can tack to the back of a door and laid it horizontal on the floor by the wall. Can you get them to assume the full puff? Does kitty walk away disinterested, bathe in the glory of its own beauty, or attempt to converse or fight with the image? Positive points can be assigned if kitty immediately recognizes himself.

- Give 5 points if he uses the mirror to preen and bathe himself. (Kind of like we humans who pass a shop window and notice in the reflection has our hair has escaped the bun, oh no!).
- Add 3 points for a kitty that recognizes that the image is himself and immediately walks away.
- If your cat is older than six months and attempts to slap at the mirror, subtract 3 points as kitty does not recognize it is his image. This indicates a lower mental age, thus, negative point worthy.
- If your cat is older than six months and still assumes the puff position when facing the mirror, subtract 5 points as your cat has not advanced to the mental age for an average cat. An average adult cat will not assume a full puff from a reflection of himself but only when he identifies a true danger.

Cat's Name	Category	Rating	Short Reason
Gabby	Non-Verbal Communication: Mirror Test	+3	Gabby looks and walks away.
Nicky	Non-Verbal Communication: Mirror Test	+5	Nicky loves the mirror and can stare at himself for hours. He thinks he is a handsome cat and he is correct.

Adult cats may also break into the puff from time to time but it is more common to see them take a stance, pull the ears back and hiss or growl. A cat that has its ears back and is showing its teeth is nothing to trifle with. This is a definite warning, not a bluff. If it's directed at you, carefully backtrack your movements and leave the kitty alone.

Figure 14-This Cat Isn't Kidding - ©Ermalaev Alexander/SHutterstock.com

Ears straight up in the air and eyes focused on a specific point is the pounce indicator. Kitty is going to spring forward and capture something. Sometimes they will even get their butts close to the ground and wiggle left and right. Some cats may also push their ears to the back position when getting ready to pounce. My cat, Butterscotch, will start to look for prey in an upright position. She'll be completely frozen with nothing but her eyes and ears moving. Once she spots something of interest, the ears move forward and she begins to slowly move her upper body forward until she is in a prone position on the ground. Now she is more than interested; she is drooling with delight. As she continues to track her prey, she gets even closer to the ground and her butt elevates slightly.

Figure 15- Cat Hunting - © Lewis Tse Pui Long/Shutterstock.com

As the prey starts to move closer Butterscotch becomes so still that she melts into the background. The prey comes within a couple of feet and ....**pounce!**; It's all over in two seconds. The capture by the neck, the kill shake and another successful hunt completed. If you get the chance to watch this, please do. A kitty in this stance mimics their larger jungle cousins and it is an amazing dance of Nature to observe. I guess it is slightly less pleasurable for the object of kitty's attention.

The Ear Wink & Head Tilt, Extreme Cuteness

An ear wink, when it goes up and down, is most often a sign of curiosity or in our house the cat is saying, "Really?" or questioning, "What are you doing?" It may also be accompanied with a tilt of the head to the side. For instance, this evening Gabby gave me the ear wink. So, I told her that I am writing a book about measuring kitty IQ. Her response was the head tilt. I am choosing to believe she was more surprised at the subject matter rather than the thought of me as an author.

Another opportunity to view the head tilt is often seen during the distribution of treats. Cats know just how much cuteness is in the head tilt and use it to their advantage. Nicky gets this look in his eyes when I am pulling a specific number of treats out of the bag. While I am extracting the treats and breaking them into smaller pieces, both cats are doing their best to prove they deserve them more. Gabby is looking very cute and twitching her ears with a "Please." Nicky is adorable, doing the head tilt from side to side in anticipation. We give them freeze dried treats which are grain-free, good for them and apparently yummy. When we reach the last pieces and there is only dust left in the bag, it can be licked from a palm or sprinkled on their food. Another use of the dust I have found is that 'Pill Pockets' can be rolled in it to make them more appealing.

Rating Opportunity: Knowing various ways to communicate with us humans is a direct sign of the intelligence level in your cat. After all, grand manipulators tend to be very smart folks. Does your cat pull at your heart strings to get what it wants? Does kitty use the head tilt during treat times or when you are eating to attempt to get more goodies?

- ☻ Give your cat 5 points if you always give in - for knowing how to manipulate the human guardian.
- ☻ Give your cat 3 points if it is successful only half of the time.

No Need to subtract points if your cat does not do this, they may learn the behavior soon, though, so keep a lookout.

Cat's Name	Category	Rating	Short Reason
Gabby	Non-Verbal Communication: The head tilt	0	Gabby doesn't think she needs to play cute for us humans so only uses this to show curiosity.
Nicky	Non-Verbal Communication: The head tilt	+3	Nicky can't help himself and does the head tilt repeatedly. This is probably justified by my hugs when he does it.

The Blink

Blinking is a way we can communicate directly with our cats. Cats blink at other cats, they blink at humans and sometimes they just blink for their own enjoyment to indicate complete contentment.

Humans, on average, blink their eyes between 15 and 20 times per minute. We blink to cleanse and distribute lubrication through our eyes as well as to protect them in situations such as wind, bright sunlight or even harsh irritants like when cutting onions. When our eyes detect something foreign, the blinking rate is increased. Just ask anyone who wears contact lenses about this.

Interestingly, there is research in progress to study the link between blinking and the area of focus in the brain. For instance, I tend to blink and look up when concentrating on a subject. For those of you who are often in meetings and may have studied body language this is a good tool to put in your back pocket if it's not already there.

Cats, on the other hand, have a different anatomy of the eye that makes the reasons we humans blink less necessary for them. A cat blink, for instinctual reasons, is more often to protect their eyes than for cleansing. You can see this during play, or when they are stalking prey during which objects may approach their eyes. Flying insects, long grass and limbs or even wind can cause kitty to blink. Have you ever noticed that most cats blink when you extend your hand to them above their face? They don't know where the hand is going and close their eyes just in case. Approach a cat with your hand from below their chin and they will reach out to see what you have for them.

Cats, like humans, also blink or close their eyes when they smell something bad. Nicky hates the smell of perfume and blinks rapidly and then closes his eyes if I approach him after a recent spritz. Cats may also blink to communicate peace, contentment or even love.

A cat who blinks is accepting your presence as non-threatening. I make it a policy never to approach a strange cat unless they blink back at me first.

Even in a pet store where they keep kitties for adoption in cages, watch the ones that blink back at you. This helps differentiate between the one that wants to go home with you and the one that either can't think of anything through the fear or may be thinking, "Please don't let that human choose me."

All of my cats respond to blinking. If I blink at Gabby, she responds with a blink back and a side-rub on my legs. If I blink at Nicky, he thinks he is getting food and starts running for the kitchen. A cat who is not blinking but staring directly at you is issuing a challenge for dominance, just like a dog would do.

Rating Opportunity: The Blink Test. Can you communicate with your cats with just your eyes? When kitty is looking at you, try a slow eye blink. What is kitty's reaction? You may have to experiment with different blinking rates. I close my eyes slowly, wait one or two seconds, then reopen them slowly. I have found this gives me the best results.

- If kitty comes directly to you as a reaction, give kitty 5 points.
- If kitty blinks back, give 3 points
- If kitty has no reaction, subtract 3 points
- If kitty continues staring (which we know means they are in competition with you for dominance) then subtract 5 points.

Try this with your friends' cats or one of the cats at the pet store. How do their reactions differ?

Cat's Name	Category	Rating	Short Reason
Gabby	Non-Verbal Communication: The blink test	+5	Gabby blinks back and immediately comes in for a hug and a kiss
Nicky	Non-Verbal Communication: The blink test	+3	Nicky blinks back a couple of times and then comes in for a hug.

Kangaroo Kitty: Protection Blinking

PM is the KIC (Kitty in Charge) and she takes her job seriously. She takes no prisoners and no excuses. As a matter of fact, the only responsibilities that lie with me are cleaning the cat pail and feeding, which are tasks too demeaning for the KIC to be bothered with. PM's rules must be followed or there will be hell to pay. She has no problem marching up to the offending kitty and swatting them good. Consider that PM is about 1/3 the size of the other cats who do not contest her role at all.

One day Falcor broke one of PM's rules. I don't actually recall what the offending action was but I was there to watch the meting out of punishment. PM walked straight up to Falcor and rose up on her hind legs so that she was standing on her haunches with paws in the air like a boxing kangaroo. Falcor immediately responded by closing his eyes and folding his ears back to the side of his head. PM hauled back and started wailing at his head. Right jab, left hook, right, left, right. She took a momentary break, Falcor opened one eye slowly to peak at her, and then she started in again. Don't feel bad for Falcor. Whatever he did, he must have had it coming and I hesitate to add that her jabs were probably like flea bites to a big tom cat like him.

Afterwards, PM walked away (or should I say strutted away) as if to say, "Take that and get on board or suffer more!" Falcor watched her leave with a confused look on his face like, "What did I do wrong?"

Tails Speak Too, 'Tattitude'

Cats use their tails in many different ways. Mothers use it as a toy to keep the kittens occupied when needed. They can also use the tail as a tool to draw the kitty where they want them to go without getting up. This comes in handy when you have 5 or 6 little kittens all trying to run in different directions. Cats can also use their tails as a weapon. Some kitties will bat at humans, another cat or a dog with their tails and, believe me, this can hurt more than you would think. And then, of course, we have the tail twitches which can mean anything from happiness or warning to nervous energy.

Even the position of the tail can indicate different messages kitty is sending. If it is wrapped around the paws in front, kitty is very comfortable and content. A tail between the legs, I am sure we all know, indicates fear, while a tail waving in the air can be a happy kitty contemplating mayhem.

45

Gabby, our female Ocicat, uses her tail in a most unusual way. While Gabby is not shy and is a pretty chatty kitty, she also communicates very effectively with her tail. Ever since she was a kitten she started to show pride in an activity by twitching her tail in a particular way that we began calling 'Tattitude' which stands for 'Tail Attitude'. Tattitude is when the cat starts with the tail straight up in the air at a 90 degree angle from the body and then proceeds to twitch her tail forward towards the ear and back to the starting position straight up in the air.

Gabby also uses her tail for accents. For instance, when Gabby catches a string and returns it, the tail goes up in the air and then twitches forward towards her nose while she is looking at you. This means, "Yes, I did that!" Gabby bats Nicky for sneezing and while walking away gives a Tattitude for "Don't mess with the Gabby; I didn't say you could sneeze." Gabby investigates a squirrel digging at the rose bush in our front and then flies up the stairs giving Tattitude the whole way. This is short for, "If I ever get my hands on that squirrel..... He'll be sorry"

Pointing out the Obvious, He did it!

Magic was an all-black female cat that was short on meows but long on the ability to use the kitty body to point out the obvious. Magic would often point to the dog whenever something went missing or awry. The dog happened to be a German shepherd named Harry who was a great dog and loved the family but was not that fond of the cat. From Harry's perspective, Magic was a little tattle tale. If the roast defrosting on the counter had somehow moved to the floor and had bite marks on it, Magic would gladly point to Harry. When the food bowl was dragged across the floor leaving kibble all over the kitchen, Magic would joyfully point to Harry. You get the point!

Figure 16- Magic Gets the Dog in Trouble

One day, I was late coming home from college and the minute I stepped in the door, I could smell that something was not right in the house. As I moved through the hallway to the living room, there was a pile of poop in the middle of the carpet. Magic was sitting on the arm of the couch waiting for me and immediately started pointing to the poop and then pointing to Harry. Harry looked at me, then at the cat and started backing up under the piano. Needless to say, the size and aromatic scents wafting in the room made it clear who the culprit was. Harry was sent outside and Magic shared a nice dinner with me in the den. End of story? Not quite.

The following day, I went to college and on my return home came in to see a repeat of what had happened the day before. There was a pile of poop in the center of the rug, the dog was cowering under the piano and there was Magic sitting on the arm of the couch pointing from the poop to the dog. Now, you might think that I would jump to the same conclusion... but the pile of poop was tiny. As a matter of fact, it was only two or three small balls and not the quantity generally seen from a German Shepherd of Harry's size. I approached the dog slowly and gave him a big hug and kiss on the forehead. I turned around to give Magic a piece of my mind but she was already gone. Not only was Magic bright

47

enough to try and place the blame on someone else but she also recognized when the gig was up.

Rating Opportunity: What cool ways of communicating do you use during interactions with your cat? Do you recognize ear or tail twitches? Does your cat lead you where she wants you to go? How does your cat tell you of her displeasure? How does she react when thrilled about a new toy?

- ❀ If your cat has a unique way of expressing itself like the Tattitude or pointing out others to blame, give kitty 5 points.
- ❀ Give 3 points if kitty meows to get your attention when another cat or human does something wrong. This is a little tattle tale kitty but a great communicator.
- ❀ If kitty gets blamed by the dog, subtract 5 points or give the dog 5 points ☺

Cat's Name	Category	Rating	Short Reason
Gabby	Non-Verbal Communication: kitty body expression.	+5	Gabby is incredibly expressive. She invented the 'Tattitude'
Nicky	Non-Verbal Communication: kitty body expression	+3	Nicky is a more subtle cat. I have to pay close attention but he does express with his tail, ears and even head nods. He is not at the level of Gabby but still greater than the average kitty.

Bird Watching

Another difference in verbal skills to observe is how cats respond to seeing prey. This is the completely different than any other vocalization, and most often observed when a kitty spies a bird. Each cat may have variations but generally they move their mouths very fast and emit a sound that is more like chatter than a standard meow. It tends to be along the lines of, "eh-eh-eh-eh-eh-eh", while the whiskers are bouncing up and down. Now, they only do this for animals they think are prey such as birds. Once I saw Gabby do this at a squirrel and had to let her know that she was too small to take on a squirrel. I bet you can guess what that paw up in the air pointed in my direction really meant!

"I believe cats to be spirits come to earth. A cat could, I believe, walk on a cloud without falling through. "

Jules Verne

Chapter 4: Fear of Noise

We are all startled to some degree, when a loud noise occurs. Actually, I tend to physically jump, which amuses my family to no end. This is common knowledge around our home, so many folks will make quiet, non-threatening sounds as they approach, to ensure my feet don't leave the floor. Thankfully, I am rating my cat's IQ in this book, not my own.

Now, we all know that cats startle easily, which for some humans make them appear nervous and scared. The truth is that cats are incredibly courageous but the courage is dependent on knowing what they are up against. In other words, they don't know what they don't know.

Vacuums

One well known cause of kitty fear is the hated vacuum. Once it turns on, every kitty in the house is running for their hidey hole such as under the bed, in the closet or someplace secret that we humans are not supposed to know about.

Figure 17- Kitty Runs from Vacuum - © ken cook/Shutterstock.com

Let's explore this from a kitty's perspective:

- A monster appliance with all kinds of hoses and nozzles hanging off it is brought out from the closet.
- An attachment or two falls off and makes a sharp clang when it hits the floor.
- The human has to wrangle with the wires and finally starts pulling one of the ends across the floor.
- Sometimes the couch or furniture is moved making a loud squeak across the floor.
- The human then does some magic to change the shape of the machine as its tall head is lowered to the floor.
- It is turned on and sounds like the ceiling is going to fall in.... arghhhhh!

Not all cats are afraid of the vacuum. Some cats even like the vacuum cleaner. If they can get over the irrational fear, cats love the suction feeling and may even stretch to allow the cleaner to access a wider area of their body. It must feel like a mini kitty massage from the way they act. Bear in mind that cats also don't mind reclining on brushes with the bristles facing up, which always looks very uncomfortable to me.

51

Our cat, PM, loves to battle the vacuum cleaner. She will watch it start up and make a few rounds of the room before she jumps into action. She approaches at a run and slaps the head of the vacuum as it's rolling across the floor. PM dances back and forth in front of it giving a good left, then right, swat while avoiding the running headlights. It is a fun experience to vacuum in our house but it does take a very long time.

Even as I write this however, the fear of vacuums is changing. Manufacturers are making new vacuums that are smaller, lighter weight, quieter or even automated. There are even commercials of a cat riding the automated robot vacuum. Hang in there kitty, the Roomba is coming!

Rating Opportunity: How does kitty react to the vacuum or other cleaning implements? Is there an initial unreasonable fear? Does the fear seem to come under control over time or does the kitty seem to get more irrational?

Here is an opportunity to add points to your cat's IQ score based on how they manage their instinctual fear response.

- If your cat is initially freaked out when you are vacuuming but has managed to control the fear and even approach the vacuum in curiosity, give kitty 5 points.
- If kitty has learned over time to accept the vacuum but watches from a safe place, give kitty 3 points.

Cat's Name	Category	Rating	Short Reason
Gabby	Fear: Vacuums	+5	Gabby initially RAN for the bed, closet or wherever she thought was safe. She learned over time to slowly approach to sniff at the vacuum but does not find it appealing and walks away.
Nicky	Fear: Vacuums	0	Nicky runs quickly from the area and cowers under the bed.

Power Tools Anyone?

Overcoming an irrational fear such as the vacuum may be just the starting point for a courageous kitty ready to conquer the unknown. Your kitty may show signs of the ability to conquer fear in small ways that can be encouraged to help kitty grow more independent. A smart cat wants to make his own choices. Cowering behind an owner's leg in extreme circumstances may be acceptable, but it is not preferred. As cats mature they need to overcome the kitty fears and become kings of the domestic jungle. The process does not take place overnight but may start with a little paw forward, two paws back, and you get the idea.

An example of a tiny courageous accomplishment is Gabby approaching the electric nail file. Gabby loves emery boards like most cats. As soon as I take out the emery board, the cats come running. Gabby is in first place, as close to my arm as possible. She watches each movement of the file across my nails and starts to sneak in for a sniff. When I extend the file fully across the nail, she bats at the exposed end in an attempt to capture the file. Eventually, I learned to bring two emery boards with me, one for Gabby to play with and one to file my nails.

Enter the electric nail file. This looks easy to do on the commercial, how could I possible get it wrong? With glee, I bring home the package and sit down in the den to extract the new girly toy. The cats gather around oohing and aahing as I explain the motorized emery board. They creep closer as I turn the carton in every direction seeking a way open it. The cats start getting nervous watching me making little to no progress. Frustrated, I pull out the sewing scissors and they both run from the room. See how smart my kitties are? I finally extract the product, insert some batteries and I am ready to go. I call the cats back into the room and we are off to the races.

I turn on the product with a buzz and Nicky immediately runs out of the room. The last sight of Nicky is his tail disappearing under the bed. Gabby, however, steps closer to see what is going on. I attempt to shape my nails and Gabby watches in anticipation of when I will let her start her own product analysis. I give in, turn it off and extend it towards her. Gabby does the sniff test, gives it a few head-butts and is ready to see it in action. I flip the switch and it starts buzzing away. Gabby takes a small step back, squares her shoulders and comes in for the close and personal examination. Gabby extends her nose so I pull back the buzzing file. Next, she extends a paw, so I slowly go in to close the distance between her nail and the buzzing file. A few short filing exercises and Gabby declares the entire process boring and walks away. I continue testing the new electronic file until I realize that I also prefer the emery board. The nail file is in some drawer along with all the other toys the cats or I no longer play with.

Hey Lady, Come Get Your Cat

If an electric file is a tiny courageous accomplishment, a power tool is a huge step forward to make the kitty roar. The average kitty rarely gets exposed to power tools, but in our recent home purchase, it has happened quite often. Between the new patio doors, cable guys and us masquerading as handymen, some project has been ongoing since the closing date. I did not think this would be a problem for the cats since they tend to 'retire to the salon', meaning they are under my bed, with the first loud noise. Much to my surprise, Gabby decided she needed to supervise the work.

If it was a matter of a cat standing and watching while workmen drilled holes in concrete or power sanded the stairs that would be amazing but Gabby went much further than just observing. She had to get close and personal.

The first time this happened, we were in a Philly apartment and the cable guy was installing all new internet and running cables. I let him know that we had cats but that he shouldn't worry as he'll likely never see them. He smiled and started setting out the equipment and measuring the area. We talked about where the main box and router should go and what should be installed in each room as we walked through the apartment. The cable guy was busy looking at the floors and ceiling to plan the wiring as we walked through all the rooms.

When we returned to the entrance area, there was Gabby sniffing the equipment and wires. I picked her up and took her back to the office area with me and returned to work. A couple of minutes later, I hear the cable guy shouting, "Hey Lady, you gotta come get your cat." Wondering what is going on, I walked back to the installation area, and there was Gabby with her nose in the hole that he had just drilled. She looked up at the cable guy and then back to the hole as if saying "Keep going, you're doing a good job so far." We both cracked up laughing while the cable guy said he had never seen a cat do anything even remotely close to that.

While that was the first time Gabby got up close and personal with a workman using power tools, it certainly wasn't the last. Gabby keeps an eye and ear out for people coming to do work on our house and she is always willing to supervise. Through the years the calls to take care of my cat have changed from picking up the remains of prey to protecting the power tools from the cat.

Rating Opportunity: Does your kitty display any courageous steps in conquering fear? It does not have to be a power tool, but should be something that would have the majority of cats running for cover. A muscle car, hammering, loud music, sirens or something else you define.

- If your cat has learned to relish or challenge the loud noise, add 5 points to your cat's IQ score.
- If you cat has adapted to the loud noise and does not cower, add 3 points to the IQ Score.

Cat's Name	Category	Rating	Short Reason
Gabby	Fear: Loud Noise	+5	Gabby supervises all activities involving power tools. She still runs from a sneeze but apparently power tools are kitty cool.
Nicky	Fear: Loud Noise	0	Nicky runs from any loud noise

Body Noises

Kitties have some very unique noises they emit. The hair ball coughing, the multiple sneezes in a row, both silent and auditory projectile vomiting, and hacking for various reasons.

Our cat Kelly liked to choke herself. She would climb inside a box, hang her head over the edge and apply pressure to her own neck until she started choking. She would straighten up, cough a bit then stick her head back on the box edge to start the entire process again. The vet said there was no physical reason for this behavior. It was just a Kelly-ism. This activity is worthy of subtracting 5 points from Kelly's score.

It is completely normal and understood that over time a cat will make various noises including a sneeze. A human sneeze on the other hand is a scary moment for the cat when the Earth may open up and swallow us all whole! If I should sneeze or, heaven forbid, fart, the cats run to the edge of the bed or out of the room and then turn to look at me with blood lust in their eyes. They return in a second or two when they think the danger has ended. A kitty fart, on the other hand, can empty a room for hours!

Rating Opportunity: This category will subtract points if Kitty is not as well versed in the activities of his human family. After all, a smart kitty would understand the human noises over time and if not able to predict them should not treat them with the same level of fear as a fire alarm.

- ☺ If your kitty has no reaction, do not subtract points.
- ☺ If your kitty scares easily and over time does not learn to detect the difference between normal and abnormal behavior, do subtract 3 points.

Cat's Name	Category	Rating	Short Reason
Gabby	Fear of Noise: Body Noises	-3	Gabby runs at every first sneeze.
Nicky	Fear of Noise: Body Noises	0	Nicky doesn't scare beyond the expected nature of a cat.

"I would like to see anyone, prophet, king or God, convince a thousand cats to do the same thing at the same time. "

Neil Gaiman

Chapter 5: Playing Expertise

A happy, healthy cat is a playing cat. Kitties have a natural curiosity that must be satisfied. It can be as simple as chasing a fly on the outside of the window, chasing their tails, following invisible insects, or coming to ask you to play with them. Our cats live in a house that caters to kitties. There is a cat penthouse or tree in most rooms and a slew of toys that seem to defy all efforts to keep them in an orderly fashion. As soon as I gather them in the corner, the cats pull them out and spread them all over the floor complaining, "Mom, stop moving my toys!"

Playing is necessary to provide stimulation, drain excess energy and let kitty know that it is a valuable member of the family. A cat that doesn't get enough play time may get cranky, sulk and then start to think evil thoughts. In my case, I can tell just by watching a cat check out my desk or purse that some evil plan is in the works. Play time can go a long way to reducing or stopping the climbing up the drapes, digging up house plants or whatever it is that your kitty knows you do not want it to do. Gabby has a talent for opening drawers and taking out all of the bras, stockings and undies. You may giggle at this but she can also start carting bras around by the straps which is just delightful when I am hosting a dinner party.

In this chapter we are going to cover hunting patterns, first, then kitty toys and reasons to play along with kitty tricks. If you prefer to skip the hunting sections, go ahead to the third section, *Play for Distraction*.

Hunting as Play Time

What we call "play time" is actually work time for kitty. For indoor cats, it is to satisfy the need for hunting live prey and to hone their killer instincts and skills. Make no mistake; a cat is one of the world's most deadly hunters.

Outdoor cats get lots of play time in actual hunting. Our best hunter was Butterscotch. Butterscotch was a petite, short-haired American domestic Calico, who terrorized the entire neighborhood wildlife. The squirrels, rabbits, and birds were all slowly disappearing. Even a new collar with tinkling bells we put on her did little to lessen her impact on other forms of life in the area. All I would hear is my mom calling, "Calla, your cat left a present for you!" and I'd have to jump into clean-up activities. My mother was not as thrilled with the back-door presents of dead birds that Butterscotch assumed she would be.

Butterscotch was amazing. We picked her up from the SPCA back in the days when you did not have to provide references, your last three tax returns, a home visit and wait weeks to adopt a pet. At that time, they were happy to get a family that wanted to open their hearts and home to be a pet guardian.

Butterscotch was 8 weeks old when we got her. She was a birthday present for me, yay me! She immediately fit right in. She slept in my bed, was the perfect companion and a very independent kitty. Actually, she was so independent that at times she didn't seem to be hungry for kibble. It took us some time to figure out exactly why.

Butterscotch knew that our back yard, since it abutted a forested area, was a kitty buffet and all she needed for the entrance fee was a healthy appetite and patience. Butterscotch watched the animals from my second floor window and made her attack plans. She knew where the animal trails all converged and times during day and night each type of animal tended to promenade. She watched for a time and then put her plans into action. She would crouch by the dark side of a bush and just wait.

Eventually, after an hour or two her prey would approach, see no sign of danger and proceed to sashay down the path. Once they got close enough... Bam! She was on them in a heartbeat and with a little kill shake of the head, it was all over except for the happy dance of the winner. The prey was so surprised that there was rarely any sign or sound of struggle.

After a year or two, Butterscotch got pregnant and we were delighted to welcome her anticipated kittens to the family. In the spring she gave birth to a litter of six; Marshmallow, Magic and four other kittens.

Butterscotch gave birth in my second floor bedroom closet and would come and go from the house by the window. She'd walk across the roof, jump to a neighboring tree and shimmy down to the ground. Sometimes, she'd even stop to snack on a tree resident if one was unlucky enough to be found. As the kittens started to open their eyes and begin exploring my bedroom, Butterscotch started to bring them food. As you have probably gotten to understand Butterscotch in this section, you might have guessed that she wasn't thinking of kibble.

Butterscotch began bringing in small dead presents to the kids to start teaching them how to hunt. Of course the kittens were too small to eat the mice or birds but they were still small cats and would bat them around until I got home to remove the evidence before my mom could find it.

Figure 18- Kitten Learns to Hunt - ©dragi52/Shutterstock.com

As the kittens started getting older, Butterscotch began bringing less dead food to her brood. First, it was mostly dead mice to partly dead mice until gradually she started bringing live mice and birds to the kittens, which is when I finally closed the window for good. Man, was she pissed. Now she had to go through the kitchen door and my mom would not let her in the house with something in her mouth... "Calla, come take care of your cat, she can't come in here with that."

Bad Kitty, Take that out of your Mouth!

Our Chicago apartment on Lake Michigan was a hoot for our cats. There was lots of wildlife around and always things to keep them occupied. My cats, PM and Tokar were indoor/outdoor kitties. They lived inside, ate inside and certainly slept inside, but they were allowed to roam outside as they liked. All the neighbors knew our cat Tokar. He was all white with long fur, very nice and friendly. His idiosyncrasy was that he preferred not to walk on concrete. Instead he would climb and jump trees or walk down the block on top of all the cars parked on the side of the street. He would jump up onto the first car trunk, walk across the body, jump to the next trunk and so on. If there was a convertible in the line, he would walk inside the interior and jump to the windshield. Nobody was mad, they all liked our Tokar and would call him over to say hello. Most of the times I went outside, he was at somebody's feet or on their car getting a quick pet. He loved the attention.

One spring weekend day, I am in my apartment and hear some kind of commotion going on outside. I look around and see PM next to me so our troublemaker is at home, this can't have anything to do with us. Then I hear a screech and some girl shouting so I jump up and go outside to see what is going on. There is a pretty, young, blond girl with a broom in her hand swatting at Tokar. I look at Tokar and he has a bird in his mouth.

The girl is incensed with tears streaming, using the broom as a weapon to hit the ground close to Tokar screaming "Stop it, let it go!" Tokar is looking at her like she is crazy. And here I come to save the day.

I approached and asked, "What do you think you are doing trying to hit my cat with a broom?" I look at the bird in Tokar's mouth and can clearly see it is twitching but has a damaged wing and obviously is not long for this life. I introduced myself and asked her name to which she responded, "Sue," and hiccupped. I tried to explain to Sue that this is Nature and this bird is in pain. The most humane thing to do is let Tokar finish the kill shake and put the poor thing out of its misery. She starts crying harder, convinced that she is doing the right thing, so I turn to Tokar and ask him to, "Drop it." Tokar drops the bird but is obviously not happy with me and we go home while the Sue is cooing over this poor bird.

Now for those who may feel bad about the bird, I have to say that Nature is not nurturing. Have you seen any wildlife documentaries or Planet Earth? For some species having 10% of the babies survive birth is a good statistic.

In any case, about three days later there is a knock at my door. I open it to find Sue there holding a paper in her hand. She wants me to pay half of the vet bill. I laughed and said, "No, but thank you for asking."

The following week, Sue brought the bird back from the vet and released it to the wild outside. That evening Tokar brought it home for dinner.

Coup-de-grace: When we had kittens, PM's litter later that spring, Sue came knocking to ask for a kitten. I said, "No, but thank you for asking."

Play for Distraction

Play time is also perfect for distracting a kitty from inappropriate behavior such as kitty fights or climbing on the drapes. You have to be careful not to immediately initiate play when you see a bad behavior or the cat will associate that bad behavior with a positive result. Instead, try and identify those times that these activities happen and head them off at the pass by starting play BEFORE they occur. Yes, this will take some research on the cat owner's part but it is well worth the effort.

Extracting the energy from kitty has benefits for the entire family. The kitty gets to enjoy the natural activities he should be doing and the humans get a satisfied cat who is content and not looking for trouble. Win-win!

Getting the Benefits of Play Time & Toys

In order to drain the excess energy, play time needs to extend until kitty says, "Stop, I've had enough. That was great!" If you're watching kitty body language, you'll know the moment. It is when kitty is lying on its side breathing heavily. I have two indicators I use to ensure our play time is successful.

1. Kitty should be exhausted and satisfied, but not to the point of bodily pain.
2. Kitty may stop play two or three times for a moment before getting another burst of energy.

Think of yourself after a game of tennis or basketball. The endorphins have been released and you feel fabulous but tired. This is exactly what we are trying to get kitty to feel.

Every cat will play with something though they might not all enjoy the same type of toy. For instance, Gabby just adores the bird on a wire that whistles, while Nicky finds them frightening and often leaves the room.

One toy that every cat I have ever met enjoys is the laser. There are two basic types of lasers. First there are the ones in an automated toy similar to a light house that sends the laser beam moving in various directions and speeds. My cats like this when it is directed to get some wall action as well as floor. What kitty can say, "No" to a chance to climb up the walls? Then there are the handheld lasers.

The laser toy I find most often requested is the handheld one that we direct in interactive play with kitty. My cats would much rather play with this laser. I searched far and wide to find one that had a persistent controller switch because my fingers got sore holding the button down for so long. If you are using this type of laser, invest in some batteries to make it more cost effective. We go through laser batteries about every three weeks.

The other toy every cat seems to love is the peacock feather. You can get these at various pet stores and my cats just go crazy for them. You can tickle the kitties' bellies and watch them laugh, or get them to jump for it. It's actually very fun to play with the long feather and they usually cost under a dollar each so it's easy to keep a stack somewhere kitty can't reach. I keep mine in a storage container by the couch. This way my kitties know when I am reaching for one and get excited. It also stops them from playing with feathers without supervision. Nicky likes to chew them, which makes me a little uneasy.

Sick Kitty Play

When you are sick or have had some type of procedure done, how do you distract yourself? Do you read, watch TV, put together a jigsaw puzzle, or read funny blogs? Cats can't do any of these things. When they get sick or come home from the vet, we don't want them wallowing in their pain. Remember the saying that 'Laughter is the best medicine?" It's true for cats, too.

What we need to do is distract kitty while the medicine has a chance to work. I know when I am sick, I feel better and have a quicker recovery when I keep busy to take my mind of the pain. So how do we do this for kitty?

Enter the laser toy. A sick kitty will usually sit in his spot, aware of the laser but not ready to commit. Eventually the kitty will start tracking the laser with his eyes. This is good; you got kitty's attention and are slowly pulling the focus from pain to toy. Finally, at some point, he will start to chase the laser. We don't want kitty running and jumping while ill but concentrating on a toy and slow motions is perfect. You have just helped in the kitty recovery. This does not mean that kitty is not in pain but you distracted him from it for some time and can do so again. It is important that kitty knows you are aware of his pain.

Did You Buy ANOTHER Toy?

We have every kind of toy produced in this century. Be it a wooden one, a wire one, a laser toy, a mat or a battery driven type. There are catnip balls, mice, carrots, spiders, cigars and doodads that I am not sure what they are supposed to be. We have crinkle balls and plastic balls with bells in them, yellow balls, green balls... you get the point. We've got balls. There are scratch post with balls, scratch posts so that the kitty can lie down, scratch posts in the corners and, of course, Gabby uses the leather bottom of my favorite chair as her personal emery board.

I purchased mats that make noise, mats that light up, mats with circling feathers and mice. And then, there are laser toys that make circles, laser toys that roll on the floor and laser toys that depend on human interaction. Any cat owner will understand when I say, the cat would rather play with the plastic bag or box the toy came in than the toy!

So why do we continue to buy the toys? There is always the chance that 'this' toy is going to be the one that they really like and can't wait to play with.

Having said that, my cats love to play and will spend every minute I devote to play time waiting for the next toy toss. Each cat has its own way of playing. Some like to chase balls and some like to bat them back at you. Some kitties can even be trained to play ping pong. Some like to chase the feather on a wire and some like the mouse on the string but the important part is that the human must be paying attention during play. If you grab a mouse on a string and leave it hanging off the chair or not making it enticing for the cat, they will most likely walk away. So the bottom line is that they are not playing with a mouse on a string, they are playing with YOU! I try to set aside at least 30 minutes each day to have kitty-focused play.

How a cat plays is tied to its mental capacity. Some play fast and some slow. Some don't seem to like to play at all and it takes time to find out what kind of movement will provoke their hunting instinct. My two current kitties are prime examples. Gabby likes fast play where the mouse or laser rushes by her and she chases it. Nicky, on the other hand, needs very slow play. If the mouse moves too quickly, he loses track of it and frustration will have him exit the game prematurely.

Rating Opportunity: How does your cat play? What types of toys are kitty's favorite?

- Give your cat 5 points if kitty can follow fast motions of the toy with great concentration.
- Give 3 points for medium quickness of play.
- Subtract 3 points if kitty lies down and makes you bring toys to it.
- Subtract 5 points if they lose visual contact easily on fast play.

Cat's Name	Category	Rating	Short Reason
Gabby	Play Expertise: Type of play	+5	Gabby likes super-fast play and attempts to anticipate where a toy will go next. Great focus and attention.
Nicky	Play Expertise: Type of play	-5	Nicky cannot track anything moving beyond a snail's pace. Bad focus and gives up easily

Toys from every day things

While I keep buying toys, the cats keep finding their favorite ones from our everyday material or clothes. For some reason, lots of cats love to chase the little pull tab you take off the milk or cream container. I think because it is small and plastic it is easy for them to manage and it can go flying off, which is a plus.

Other everyday items in our house that the cats love are wine corks. I have yet to meet a kitty that will not chase a cork. They are small, roll around the floor and can bounce off walls.

Gabby is the only kitty I have had that is addicted to strings. Anything that can be interpreted as a string is a toy to her. My hair scrunchies, the shoulder straps on bathing suits, the little clear plastic loops on dresses so they don't fall off the hanger and others.

What makes Gabby unique is not the fact that she plays with strings but HOW she plays with them. The minute Gabby has captured a string she starts giving the 'Look at me!" meow. She meows with the string in her mouth the entire way over to you and then drops it next to your feet so you can throw it. As soon as she catches it, the meowing starts back up until she can place it at your feet once again. And the game of fetch continues.

Gabby is also a play initiator. When she thinks it is time to play, the play meow starts (this is a distinct vocalization only for strings) and she either brings the string to you or calls for you to come join her. Her timing for play does not take into account human activities. It is solely dependent on Gabby's desire. I can't count the number of times her call for string play, which is pretty loud, has interrupted dinner parties. Guests want to know what Gabby is asking for. When I explain, they walk over to see her hovering over the string meowing and call it 'adorable'. They might not think it is so 'adorable' at 3:00 am.

Gabby loves her strings so much that she carts them to bed. I can't tell you how many times I have rolled over in discomfort to find a string underneath me. Videos of string catches, return and meows along way are posted on or Facebook page.

Kitty Tricks

Is the kitty circus in town? It is in our house. Cats do love to do tricks. Not all cats, though. It was beneath Gabby and PM to consider tricks but my male kitties just love them. Nicky jumps through hoops, literally. Anything to get a treat ☺

It all started when a friend gave us a book on how to train your cat which came with a clicker. After a little experimentation I found that Nicky would come to any place I pointed to with the clicker. That led to building hoops out of my nephew's train tracks and placing chairs apart to get him to jump from one hoop through another. The most interesting part was that Nicky loved to do this for company or the camera. Anyone who thinks a pet does not know when they are being captured on video is mistaken. They love it and will pose quite often. Gabby is a ham!

Rating Opportunity: Have you taught your cat any tricks? Try getting kitty to jump to a ledge on the cat tree or a window-sill. The first couple of times might require a treat for reinforcement but once the action is second nature a simple hug or 'Good boy' will do just as well.

- Give your cat 5 points if it is capable of doing astounding tricks in a repeatable and reproducible fashion.
- Give your cat 3 points if it is learning tricks but may not be successful all the time.

Cat's Name	Category	Rating	Short Reason
Gabby	Play Expertise: Kitty tricks	0	Gabby thinks tricks are demeaning and is seeing her lawyer.
Nicky	Play Expertise: Type of play	+5	Nicky loves doing all kinds of tricks and is best in front of the camera or company

And When Play is Inappropriate

When my nephew, Blaise, was young, we would often watch him during the weekends. Blaise was a little older than three and loved spending time with our two new kittens, Alex and Gabrielle. Blaise and I would play astronaut where we would visit different planets, hang out in our astronaut outfits and camp out in the spaceship, a big tent, in the living room.

Figure 19- Alex Checks out the Astronauts

While we were launching and landing our capsule, looking at moon rocks or watching cartoons, the cats would observe, try and get in the spaceship with us and have fun chasing us around the house.

Figure 20- Alex Wants Launch

As anyone with a child can guess, inevitably a tantrum ensues with the crying, the moon rock flying across the room and the disruption of playtime. Our method of handling this is the time-out. I would point to the corner of the room and with much reluctance and mumbling, Blaise would make his way to the corner. Of course, with the crying, flying objects and whining, the cats had also fled under couches or behind the TV. I really never considered that these time-outs could be an education for the cats or have lasting effects.

Once the time-out period was completed, play would recommence amidst much laughter, new space travels and sounds of capsule landings.

Once during a workday, I was distracted from a conference call by the sounds of a kitty fight. I went into the living room and there was Gabby licking her paw and Alex staring at the floor with a guilty look. Alex turned to me and I didn't even think twice but pointed to the corner and said "Time-out." Believe it or not he put his head down and slowly walked to the corner, the same corner Blaise sits at for his time-out.

He sat facing the wall until I said, "Okay, time-out is done" when he ran back to me ready to play. Honestly, I almost wet my pants laughing silently. I never guessed that he had paid attention to my interaction with Blaise so closely that he recognized when I mandated the time-out. This cat learned from observing human behavior over time. Very crafty kitty!

Rating Opportunity: Here is an opportunity to add points to your cat's IQ measurement

- If you have noticed any exceptionally insightful behavior give 3 or 5 points as deserved. Be honest and prepared to defend the extra points!

Cat's Name	Category	Rating	Short Reason
Gabby	Play Expertise: Extra Credits	0	None
Nicky	Play Expertise: Extra Credit	+5	Nicky is Alex's cousin and has self-enforced his own timeout periods

"It is difficult to obtain the friendship of a cat. It is a philosophical animal... one that does not place its affections thoughtlessly."

Theophile Gautier

Chapter 6: Boundary Acknowledgment

Yes, this goes both ways. My cats know what is mine that they are not supposed to touch, and they let me know, in no uncertain terms what they consider sacrosanct that I am not allowed to interfere with. Let's look a little more closely at these two types of boundaries.

Hey, that's mine!

I was downstairs watching TV in the den and both kitties were taking cat naps, one on the couch next to me and my boy in the kitty condo in the corner. I noticed that the cat toys that we attempt to localize in and around the tree were now strewn across the den and climbing up the stairs. I started at the base of the condo and began sorting the toys by those they play with and those they show no interest in. In the 'no interest' pile I also stacked the older catnip toys. Slowly, I started adding the discarded pile to the waste basket by my desk. Sounds normal so far, right?

Eventually I made my way through the den and started collecting those on the stairs. While I was doing this, Gabby started going through the ones in the waste basket, pulling out the ones she still wanted. Not only did she rescue them from the garbage but she took them all the way upstairs to the bedroom and left them under the bed. She told me exactly where the boundary exists.

Figure 21-Gabby Knocks Over the Bag to Save String

Since then when I do the toy clean up, I sort them into two piles and let her loot through the 'discard' pile before I throw them out. My brother would say that Gabby has no idea what the 'discard' pile implies but I beg to differ, and it works for us.

Rating Opportunity: How do you clean up old toys?

- 🐾 If your kitty runs through the recycle pile like they do in my house, give kitty 5 points.
- 🐾 If you don't buy kitty toys and they 'play' with your favorite items, subtract points from your own IQ measurement.

Cat's Name	Category	Rating	Short Reason
Gabby	Boundaries: Mine	+5	Gabby knows what is no longer of interest and has no problems saying goodbye but "Don't take 'that' one!"
Nicky	Boundaries: Mine	0	Nicky doesn't seem to make attachments to inanimate objects other than the laser.

What's yours is mine

Now, going in the other direction of, "This belongs to human, do not touch" things are less clear. For instance, my bed really belongs to the cats and they allow me, in their consideration, a space to occupy for sleep. In other words, everything that is theirs is theirs and everything that is mine is theirs. There are exceptions to this rule such as my computer. They all know that the laptop is completely off limits but.... it did take some educating on both sides.

Figure 22-Kitty Stopping Work @merkulovstudio\Shutterstock.com

After finding the keyboard's 'A' and 'X' keys on the floor, I had to learn not use a screen saver with a mouse or other animation that draws them in and they had to learn that mommy would not be happy if a paw hit a keyboard. The boundary is set with a firm "No" and the calm removal of kitty from the area. Repeat as often as needed.

We have a couple of non-negotiable boundaries with the cats, the most important one being the counter tops. This is to protect them as well as us. We have a very active household with multiple 'chefs' at work so as much as I scream and cajole about leaving out knives and dangerous items, apparently cats are easier to train then other humans.

Besides the inadvertent dangers left behind from humans, we don't want the cats on the counters for sanitary purposes. Let's put it this way, I wouldn't want my shoes on the surface I am using to prepare food and I don't want any little kitty paws there either. Kitchen and bathroom countertops however are different, according to cats. While my fur balls may rarely attempt to approach the kitchen ones, they love the counters in the bathroom.

Measure Your Cat's IQ

Cats usually like to watch the humans brush teeth, put on makeup, or shave. The do tend to run away when the hair dryer comes out.

Do you ever wonder what the cat is thinking when he watches you groom? Does he think we waste a lot of time and effort when a good tongue bath would be more effective and enjoyable?

Rating Opportunity: Can you name 3 boundaries that you have identified for your kitty to abide by? Do they pay attention or do as they please?

Our three boundaries are the following:

1. Kitchen counters
2. Computer area
3. Human food

Now rate the cat's understanding and his following of your boundaries.

- ❀ If the cat respects your boundaries give kitty 5 points.
- ❀ Give kitty 3 points if you periodically find him crossing the boundary and have to re-enforce
- ❀ If the cats do not respect your boundaries, subtract 3 points from your own personal IQ score.
- ❀ If you have no boundaries with the cat at all, subtract 5 points from your own personal IQ score.

Cat's Name	Category	Rating	Short Reason
Gabby	Boundaries: Yours	+3	Gabby recognizes boundaries but doesn't like them. It is all about the Gabby.
Nicky	Boundaries: Yours	+5	Nicky Is very aware of what is Gabby's, what is "Humans'" and that he can use the rest. Nicky will never approach the computer or a plate of food but I have caught him on the kitchen counter.

Halloween Observer

Falcor used to love sitting on the vanity in the bathroom whenever I was in the room. He loved to watch me getting ready and just had to see what mommy was up to.

One Halloween I decided to dress up as a cat. I had prepared some home-made ears by attaching cardboard cut-outs to a headband and was in the bathroom getting ready with Falcor watching from the counter. I started applying liquid liner to my eyes which was an extreme version of my daily eye wear. Falcor started cocking his head from side to side wondering what I was doing. Then I colored the tip of my nose pink with black outline and used a brow pencil to create whiskers. It was looking pretty good if I may say so myself, and Falcor started twitching his ears back and forth.

I put the coup de grace in place by putting my hair into a ponytail and putting the headband with ears on top of my head. Falcor started hissing at the mirror.

Figure 23- Cat Hissing at Woman Cat

I went into the living room and tested the other two cats. No response, but every time I put the ears on in front of Falcor, he would hiss. I wound up taking the ears with me under my coat to put on outside where it was safe. Now I am hiding my clothing from my cats... which brings back memories of wearing layers to hide the 'indecent' one from my mother ☺

Rating opportunity: Have you noticed your cats looking at you funny when you are wearing a different hat or changing your hair style? Cats are very visual. Butterscotch actually attacked our poodle after he was shaved by the vet. He looked like a different dog and she didn't allow him to get close enough for the smell test. Do some experimenting with your kitty. Try some fun ways of changing your hairstyle or accessorizing with hats with horns, put your hair straight up into a top ponytail, put on a wig or something else outlandish. The intelligent kitty will recognize that it is still you.

- ❀ If Kitty reacts to the change with head-butt or body rub, give kitty 5 points.
- ❀ Give kitty 3 points if it recognizes you but doesn't approach. In my house this is a "Mom is doing crazy stuff again."
- ❀ Subtract 3 points if kitty runs away scared.
- ❀ Hissing will subtract 5 points.

Cat's Name	Category	Rating	Short Reason
Gabby	Boundaries: Observations	0	Gabby doesn't even take a second glance if I have a hat on, a wig or change my hair color.
Nicky	Boundaries: Observations	-3	Nicky is extremely visual and notices a haircut. Most responses are positive but he will run away if he's unsure what I am ☺

That is Mom's Pillow

Cats have definitive boundaries between themselves and other animals as well. Anyone with a multi cat or dog household will verify this. There are things a cat will share with me but not with another cat. One example of this is my pillow. Gabby insists on taking cat naps on the left side pillow, the side that I prefer. If Nicky or another human attempts to use this pillow, Gabby will definitely attack. This happened to my sister-in-law who was testing out my new tempur-pedic adjustable bed. She, unfortunately, reclined on my side of the bed and was testing the adjustments and massaging options. Gabby came right up and smacked her on the face. The translation is close to "Get off my pillow!" Everyone in the family has a healthy fear of Gabby. If Nicky was on that pillow it would precipitate the same response.

Eating Boundaries

Nicky has a favorite shelf on the cat condo and he is more prone to share his toys than Gabby. Food on the other hand is where he draws the line. Nicky and Gabby share a water bowl but have separate food bowls. Gabby likes chicken or tuna flavors and prefers hard food or gravy overload in wet food. Nicky only likes minced turkey and will eat almost nothing else. That is, in his bowl it HAS to be minced turkey, but given the opportunity he will eat anything that is in Gabby's bowl. I feed them together; putting down the bowls and watching the race ensue. Nicky rushes to eat his portion so he can go grab whatever is left in Gabby's. A couple of mouthfuls and then he sneaks a peak to see how quickly Gabby is working.

When his bowl is empty, he starts making his way to Gabby's. All I have to say is, "Nicky, your own bowl please" and he stops and just watches her eat. On the other hand, if I am not in the room, he will nose her out of the way. What a pig!

Rating Opportunity: Does your kitty listen to you? Does kitty understand the word "No", or does he practice 'selective hearing'?

- 🐾 If your kitty listens every time you say, "No", give kitty 5 points.
- 🐾 If he listens only when you're watching, give him 3 points.
- 🐾 If kitty starts to slowly inch towards the object he is not supposed to touch, subtract 3 points.
- 🐾 If he pays you no mind at all and races to the object, it is your choice to subtract 5 points from either Kitty's IQ score or yours.

Cat's Name	Category	Rating	Short Reason
Gabby	Boundaries: Respecting 'NO'	+3	Gabby is like most of my female cats, they don't like the word 'No'. She will give me a dirty look but listens.
Nicky	Boundaries: Respecting 'NO'	+3	Nicky when food is present, will only behave when I am there. If I leave or turn around, he will eat all the other cat's food. If food is not part of the equation, he always understands and respects a 'No'.

> *"There are two means of refuge from the miseries of life: music and cats."*

Albert Schweitzer

Chapter 7: Don't Bother Hiding That

Did you seriously think kitty can't find where you hid the good stuff? The next time you can't find your car keys or cell phone, just ask the cat! Cats know where everything is, the regular storage places as well as those special hiding places you think are so secretive or sneaky. Come on, you cannot out-sneak a cat.

I Know Where the Treats Are

Cats watch everything even when they appear to be 'cat napping'. It is hard for a simple human to pull one over on the little fur ball. Last night I was giving Gabby and Nicky treats at play time and afterwards, when they were both splayed out on the floor in play comas, I went and put the treats away in the top bureau drawer in my bedroom. About an hour later, I caught Nicky trying to open the drawer. He was on the top near the TV and attempting to pull up the knob. I took the treats downstairs where I normally keep them in an airtight container that even some animals with thumbs can't open.

There is a video making the rounds on YouTube in which a team of two cats collaborated to pull a frozen salmon steak out of the freezer and ate it once it was defrosted. Think about this.

- These cats made a common goal
- Planned the heist
- Waited patiently for the time it took the salmon to defrost.

I think these two were a better and more effective team than my developers at work. What gave these two kitties away was the wet floor they left behind that incented the owners to put a camera in place to catch them in the act. I classify these two as top IQ 'Devilish Genius' cats!

When Mom and Dad are at Work, Let's ...

When I lived in Chicago, I had three cats who loved their catnip. I would lay down newspaper and sprinkle catnip over it. All three cats would slowly approach each time as if this was a new activity or, perhaps, a trick. As soon as one cat would take a nibble, the rest would start digging in. They would have a ball, rolling around, nibbling clinging leaves from each other and even taking running leaps and sliding into the middle. As you might guess, even with my attempt to contain the catnip, it would end up spread from wall to wall across my living room. Once they had their fill, the catnip was mostly gone and they would finally crash wherever they ended up, the boys on their backs with paws up in the air and the girl on her side fully stretched out. This is the catnip coma!

I kept the tin of catnip inside an airtight plastic bowl (Similar to the kind of container that wonton soup comes in for take-out orders from our favorite Chinese restaurant) that I struggled each time to open. I kept the bowl at the very top of a seven foot bookcase that was placed all on its own in the middle of the room. This, I thought, was a very safe location as even I had to ask my husband to help or use a stool to get it down. Silly me.

One day I came home from work and knew right away that something was not right. Not a single cat was waiting to greet me, which has never happened. There is always at least one cat waiting to complain. They can complain about lots of things. "I'm hungry", "Where were you?", "There is a mess in the pail", and of course they complain about each other... "He wouldn't let me have my favorite spot in the sun"; "She hissed at me for absolutely no reason", "Why can't I be a single child?" This time there was no welcome and it was eerily quiet.

I stepped through the hallway and there in the middle of the living room were all three cats huddled around some kind of mess. I came closer and was shocked. One of them, (I suspect Tokar), jumped to the top of the library shelf, knocked down the catnip bowl and then they dedicated little kitty teeth to tearing apart the plastic bowl. It was no more.

Figure 24-Catnip © http://slaplaughter.danoah.com/who-can-f-it-up-faster-food-edition/2/

There was a pile of small plastic bits scattered everywhere, a big mountain of catnip in the center and three bad kitties stoned out of their minds. I fell to the floor, laughing so hard there were tears streaming down my cheeks. My little girl picked her head up an inch off the floor and squeaked at me to say, "Yeah, I know. Can we talk about this later?" and then she passed right out.

Now, this might not seem to be so much about intelligence but I can appreciate the planning, reasoning, and execution of this feat, and the satisfaction of a job well done by a team. I would rate this as Psycho

Superior although I'm not quite sure out of the three of them who was Psycho and who was Superior!

Rating Opportunity: What kinds of things do you hide from your cat? Do they know where the stash is located? Have you ever found them uncovering the goodies? Even better, does your cat hide things from you? Do you know where he stashes his goodies?

- ☻ Give kitty 5 points if he has found your secret stash,
- ☻ Give 3 points if he knows where it is but can't get into it.
- ☻ Subtract points if kitty doesn't care or is ambivalent.

Cat's Name	Category	Rating	Short Reason
Gabby	Hidden Objects: Secret Stash	+3	Gabby knows where the stash is but hasn't yet tried to break the lock.
Nicky	Hidden Objects: Secret Stash	+5	Nicky not only knows where the stash is but studies all my new hiding places. He has been caught trying to open the doors.

Cats Hide Things Too!

Before we leave the hiding chapter, I think it is prudent to mention how kitty hides objects from us humans too. As in boundaries, hiding objects goes two ways. There are items we hide from kitty, usually for their protection, and there are items kitty hides from us.

Let me start the story with a statement, Falcor is a collector. He doesn't collect baseball cards, stamps or something cool like that. As a matter of fact his collections are spontaneous and focus on whatever the day brings him. One day he will collect flower petals, which means I will get a mountain of flower petals in the center of my living room. The next day he may collect leaves and give me a mountain of those as well.

We lived in Chicago in an apartment complex right on the lake. It was a ground floor apartment but because it was lake side, it was lower than most buildings I have lived in. Our window in the living room was at ground level. We would leave the windows open when at home so the cats could climb up the couch and out the window easily. On a lovely Sunday afternoon my husband would watch football, I would read on the couch and the cats would climb over us to go in and out through the window.

Enter the collector. While I reclined with a good book, Falcor would jump over me on his way to explore what the universe had to offer that day. Eventually, his interest was piqued by something so he'd grab it in his mouth to cart home. He came back through the window with his offering, showed it to me for approval, and upon a "Good boy!" would leave it on the rug to go collect more. At the end of the day I would take out a garbage bag, heave the mountain of whatever he had brought that day in and vacuum the rug. One day it was petals, the next was leaves, sometimes it was twigs but it was whatever caught his eye and he thought was pretty. He was most interested in leaves and would sometimes even bring similar shapes or colors.

One Saturday, as winter was approaching I fell asleep. When I woke up there was a pile of feathers on the rug. Falcor had never collected feathers before but the other cats, PM and Tokar didn't seem to think anything of it so I cleaned up as usual, made dinner and went to bed. The following day was a Sunday and we were in full football mode. The game was on, cold beers were open and everyone was having fun. I thought I heard a strange noise and asked my husband, but he said hadn't heard anything suspicious. We continued talking and backseat quarterbacking the game until I heard it again. This time I muted the TV and then my husband heard it to. After some looking around, I was shocked to find a live pigeon sitting in the corner of the living room behind the chair.

Now my mind was spinning. Yesterday I had cleaned up feathers, and now here was a partially bald bird in my house. Falcor had hid a bird in the house to play with later. And by the way, this bird was bigger than any of my cats. It clicked. I looked at Falcor who in turn looked at the floor, the ceiling, his mom, my husband…. He looked everywhere except at me or the bird. Then things started to move at warp speed. Tokar, the father, heard the noise and came in drooling at the prospect of Pigeon a La Football. PM came in and said, "I doubt mom is going to like this one." My husband ran to get my oven mitts to grab the pigeon and I ran to save my oven mitts. We each had our own objective.

Eventually, we got the pigeon outside without the cats being present. It took off happily to wherever pigeons rest up from kitty induced trauma and our cats were not pleased with us. Happy Sunday!

"Cats seem to go on the principle that it never does any harm to ask for what you want. "

Joseph Wood

Chapter 8: Eating Patterns & Food Cravings

Cats have just as many peculiarities about food and eating as we humans do. Think about the last time you ate dinner with a group of people. Did they all eat the same way or was each person's eating behavior unique? Who was the first one done? Who held both the fork and the knife at the same time? Did everyone cut their protein to the same size? Who added salt or some other spice or flavoring? Who mixed all the dinner components together versus who ate each independently? Some folks don't even like the different types of food touching each other on the plate. Why should cats be different?

We will discuss some non-pet prepared foods in this chapter. Be aware that some human food can be dangerous to kitty. See the note in the *Putting It All Together and What Does It Mean* chapter where we list some of those foods to avoid sharing with kitty.

Clean Up After Yourself

No matter how my cats eat, the one thing they all have in common is that they are little pigs. Given the opportunity, there will be food all over the floor, the plate, their noses and, somehow, the kitchen cabinets. Gabby likes to eat moving her face from side to side using her back teeth to chew the food into tiny pieces before she swallows. Sometimes the side to side motion causes food to go flying across the kitchen. I have since found some great pet food and water bowl holders that have silicon borders that the bowls sit in. This goes a long way to protecting the floor area from food spills. It also stops the cats from dragging the plates all over the kitchen but I have yet to find anything to protect the walls.

My first Somali cat, Alex, was truly surprising. First of all, he may be the most gorgeous cat I have ever seen but, then again, I am biased. Secondly, he was the first cat we ever had who cleaned his plate. I don't mean that he finished his food; I mean he literally swept the floor by the plate.

Figure 25- Alex, Our Little Cleaner

Alex was not really sweeping the floor to clean it; instead he is following an instinctual behavior called 'Food Caching'. This is when cats cover up their food so predators can't find what they want to finish later or won't be able to track where kitty has been.

Interestingly, they may not have learned this from their mother cat but this knowledge may be passed through genetics and is a shared characteristic among felines including the big cats such as lions and tigers. This makes for an interesting addition to nature versus nurture discussion, doesn't it? ☺

Rating Opportunity: How does your cat eat? Is he a little piglet like my fur balls or is he meticulously neat like that cat on the commercial that eats from a crystal glass? Does he lick his plate clean or always leave some food in it for later? Does he exhibit any activity that could be part of 'Food caching'?

- ☙ Give kitty 5 points if there are signs of food caching such as sweeping by the bowl.
- ☙ Give 3 points if kitty generally leaves his plate empty to prepare for the next meal.

Cat's Name	Category	Rating	Short Reason
Gabby	Food: Food Caching Stash	0	Gabby, makes a mess when eating and doesn't seem to acknowledge that there will be a need to eat again later.
Nicky	Food: Food Caching	+5	Nicky began 'food caching' as a small kitten and continues to this day

Sit Down, Relax, and Eat:

Every cat does, indeed, have a different way of eating. Some stand up and inhale their food, some sit calmly and eat at a steady pace while still others lie down and eat at their leisure.

One of our cats, named Nestle Crunch Bar used to eat slouched down and humming. It wasn't a purr or a growl it was more of a hum as in 'mum-mum-mum-mum-um, mum-mum-mum'. It was extremely funny. Friends would come over hoping to see him eat. He hummed the entire way through each meal. The dog would keep glancing at Nestle as if to say, "What is wrong with this picture?"

Butterscotch would eat standing up, which I assume was so that she could protect or move her food if competition appeared. Falcor ate his meals lying down and took his time to savor every bite. In case you are wondering, he was a big, healthy boy. PM, Falcor's mother ate crouched down at a constant pace until all the food was gone. Gabby doesn't eat, she noshes. Three bites of kibble here, five pieces of kibble there. She rarely eats what I would consider a full meal. Our vet says she is very healthy with a perfect, lithe, kitty body. Magic would not eat unless a human was in the kitchen with her. Reminds me of a friend who claims she doesn't like to eat alone. On the other hand, I love to go to dinner by myself, meaning me and the paper. It is often the only time I get to read a newspaper all the way through.

We used to feed our cats wet food periodically and hard food that was always present to nosh on as desired. That was until Nicky came along. Nicky, is our Somali who makes every woman who walks in the door say "Aww. That is the most gorgeous cat." Gabby with her leopard spots and trim little panther body is fodder for the men but the women just love Nicky's long fluffy hair, gray and beige coloring and huge pools of green/gold eyes.

In any case, no matter how gorgeous he is, Nicky is lacking the 'Off' button. By 'Off' button, I mean that little voice in his head that says, "I am full." Nicky will eat, and eat and eat until he is so full he throws up … and then he eats again. Kind of like college boys with alcohol.

Once we realized the issue, we started doing research and it turns out that other kitties lack an eating 'Off' button, too. The most often quoted advice was to feed the cat in a bowl and spread the food around so that it takes them longer to eat.

For Nicky, this does not work. That cat can clean the bottom of any plate, bowl or serving dish in record time and will still go upchuck on my favorite carpet. What works for us is reducing the food given to about a tablespoon at a time. This means we do feed him more often but it stays down. When Nicky does start to make throw up noises, I tell him "You ate it, you keep it" and he stops right away.

One of the side benefits of feeding Nicky smaller meals more often is that it keeps his weight constant, which is healthier for an altered male. It makes perfect sense when you consider that all the diets advertised lately put people on a schedule of eating high protein foods about every third hour. Who would have guessed we would stumble upon the same idea for our cat?!

Rating Opportunity: Does your cat eat in a relaxed manner and enjoy his food or is he poised to run at the first noise? Does kitty keep the food down or are you often following kitty with paper towels?

* Give your kitty positive points for enjoying food and keeping it.
* Subtract points for the anxious eater or the temporary grazer.

Cat's Name	Category	Rating	Short Reason
Gabby	Food Eating Patterns :	-3	Gabby is a very nervous eater. Half the times her back paw is extended for instant retreat from the food area.
Nicky	Food Eating Patterns :	+3	Nicky scores a 3 in this category. He had issues with consistent regurgitation of food but this has been mostly resolved with the change in feeding frequency.

Please Eat

Cats have sophisticated taste for those who are expected to live and thrive on dry food. Or, is it us humans who are certain that kitty needs endless flavors made in various ways including: minced, diced, shredded, in gravy, in sauce, pate and the ever so unpopular, raw. A new cat owner could literally spend hours in the pet store trying to figure out what the best diet is.

Cats however, have their own ideas and since they can't actually read the cans may not be on the same page with the experts as to what is best for them. Is there any cat owner who at one time or another has not opened can after can after can, begging kitty to, "Please eat!"? Are they laughing at us?

Figure 26-Kitty Says "Talk to the Paw" ©Eric isselee/Shutterstock.com

I try to keep all my cats on a strict diet of only grain-free food that meets their specific nutritional needs but there are times when kitty gets to try human food. Some of my cats have had very eccentric cravings to say the least.

Pizza Anyone?

Like most families, we love pizza and, living in NYC, there were boat loads of really good pizza joints that delivered. We would get pizza often and, depending on who was home, could get a number of pies with a wide range of toppings.

One day we were all joking around and eating pizza and my mom gave our young cat PM a small piece of mushroom. PM loved it. She ate it immediately and was begging for more. After that, every time we ordered pizza we had to have half a small pie with mushrooms. None of my other cats like mushrooms, thank goodness, because I am not too fond of them myself ☺

PM also liked Jalapenos. Please don't ask me how we found this out but she just loved them. Would lick away with tears streaming from her eyes but kept on going.

PM Has Her Own Pint of Ice Cream

When I was attending college in New York, PM and I lived down in the village in a small 2 bedroom we shared with my brother. Just like any college age siblings, we each had our own group of friends, activities and mostly saw each other on weekends aside from the occasional "Hello" in the hallway. As a college kid, money was tight and I would bring home half my meals from dinner for lunch the following day. My brother considered anything found in the fridge to be common property and I would find my take out boxes empty except for a used fork left for me. This really used to tick me off and I was always screaming at him to stop taking my food... with little luck.

One day I picked up a pint of ice cream, Haagen-Dazs rum raisin to be precise. I was eating it with a spoon on my bed watching Star Trek (yes, I am a trekkie) when PM asked to have a taste. I got a napkin and put a little dot of ice cream on it. She loved it, more than mushrooms!

After that, I would pick up two little cups of rum raisin and PM and I would pig out together. I would open hers and put it on the floor while I ate my own cup with a spoon. I only eat about three or four spoons at a time so two cups would last each of us for a couple of servings. PM liked to eat around the raisins and then periodically eat a bunch of them at once. I would write 'PM' on one of the cups to tell the difference.

Figure 27- Kitty Get Her Own Ice Cream

One day, I was studying at my desk when my brother came in and leaned against my door with a silly grin on his face. He said, "I eat your food because you bring the best stuff home" and then proceeded to put a big spoon of ice cream is his mouth. He ate a couple of spoons and continued with, "Thanks for the treat". I responded with, "Don't thank me, thank PM". He looked at the cup, looked at me, looked at the cat and back at the cup. "You give her a spoon in a bowl right?" he asked. With a grin I replied, 'Why no, that's her cup that she licks from directly". My brother ran to the sink making some pretty cool choking noises and PM and I high fived each other. In case you are wondering, this did not resolve my take-out food box disappearance but ice cream was left alone from then on.

Did I Hear Someone Say Martini?
Before you start thinking the worst, no, we do not give alcohol to our cats. However, I have heard of both cat and dog owners giving some small libations to their pets. Beer, particularly I understand. I don't judge others on this account, I am just too selfish to share my booze...not to mention that cats are already 3 sheets to the wind in their natural state, if you know what I mean.

One day I was relaxing after work and made myself the perfect martini with three olives. I left it for just a moment while I went back to the kitchen for some cheese, crackers and pepperoni. I was going to have a very good night! When I got back to the den, there was Gabby with her entire paw in my martini. I shouted, 'Gabby, what on Earth are you doing?' She looked up at me, did a last swat to toss an olive to the floor and ran to the olive right away. I thought she was after my vodka but little did I know that the garnish was the objective all along.

As I watched in wonder, Gabby started licking the olive across the carpet. All I was thinking was how heavy the carpet shampoo machine was going to be to lug upstairs. Selfish moment again, along with the thought, that my martini was no longer drinkable. Then Gabby started rubbing her whole body on the olive, similar to her actions with catnip.

Now, it started to make sense. All those times that Gabby stays in the kitchen while I am cooking happen to be when I am using olive oil. The tuna fish she likes is the one that I spike with olives. That's it, it's OLIVES! Now whenever I make a martini, I bring a separate olive along just for Gabby and my glass stays safe from prying kitty paws.

Rating Opportunity: Does your kitty crave something other than kibble? What kind of foods do you let them try? Now, I am not recommending giving cats human food. The fact that cats don't beg while we are eating is a plus in my book. Most pets do wind up nibbling on something their owners eat.

- Give your cat 5 points if he loves something truly unique such as olives.
- Give 3 points for standard foods like salmon, tuna or turkey. .

Note of caution: Some human foods are dangerous or even deadly for pets. Be sure you check the toxicity.

Cat's Name	Category	Rating	Short Reason
Gabby	Food Cravings: Cuisine	+5	Gabby is a true connoisseur. She likes olive, nibbles them and rolls around on top of them.
Nicky	Food Cravings: Cuisine	+3	Nicky eats mainly cat food but he is a sucker for fresh turkey

"Do our cats name us? My former husband swore that Humphrey and Dolly and Bean Blossom called me The Big Hamburger. "

Eleanora Walker

Chapter 9: Name Recognition

It will be no surprise to any pet owner that cats do indeed know their names. Not only their own names but those of the humans and other pets and may even remember the names of those who have passed away.

Test this with your cat. Before calling kitty by his own name, use the same exact tone and inflection but call a name not associated with anyone in the family. Try a new name that has never been spoken in the house before and see what happens. Note what happens and then do the same test but this time using the kitty's name. We'll circle back to this in the scoring area.

Mom, I'm Not Johnny!

In a house with more than one cat it is important to call the cat by the correct name. When you look at one cat and call it by the other's name, they give you a look like 'What is mommy drinking now?'

PM, our Korat kitty, not only knew her own name but recognized the names we gave to each of her kittens. She birthed her kittens in my shirt drawer at the beginning of spring. When she started labor, she simply opened the bottom drawer, pulled out half of the t-shirts and made herself a nice cozy den to bear the kittens. I found out by entering the bedroom to see my clothes all over the floor and saw her panting on her side. I have heard that cats like to give birth alone and are very protective

101

of the kittens from human approach but PM was the opposite. As soon as she saw me enter, she meowed to get me to come over and reached out to touch my hand. I watched the entire birthing process from beginning to end and as each kitten was born, she would clean the kitten and then nose it over to my hand so I could pick it up and hold it gently while it wriggled around in my palm. I held each kitten, gave it a little smell and put it back down next to PM as she started bringing the next kitten to the world. PM purred through the entire process which took a little more than two hours. About a week later, she moved the kittens to our bedroom bookcase. I guess she took after her human mother with a love of books.

Back to the reason this story belongs in this chapter of the book. Within a week we had developed names for each kitten. Falcor was the first one born and made sure to consume the colostrum from each nipple before the other kittens could get there. He was about twice the size of the other kittens within a couple of days. He was all white, kitten fluffy, and looked like the dragon from The Never Ending Story, hence the name Falcor. T2 (Terminator) was the next kitten born. Another male, also all white but had a little gray yarmulke on the top of this head. Confidentially, he was my favorite and the one I wanted to keep. All the other kittens got representative names as well.

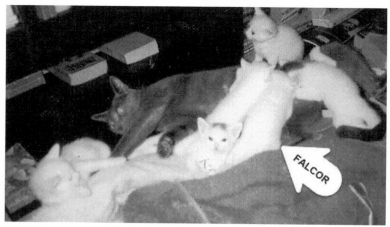

Figure 28- PM with her kittens

As the early weeks passed and the kittens started exploring and getting into trouble, all I'd have to do is ask PM, 'Where is Falcor?' She'd look around and either point him out or go track him down and bring him back by the scruff of his neck.

Thus I have seen evidence that cats know not only their own name but those of the other cats, even new additions like kittens. They also recognize the names of other household pets like the dog, birds and rabbits.

A cat associates us humans not only with our names but with our roles as well. For instance, Gabby knows me as 'Calla' or 'Mommy'. She probably has a couple of other choice words for me as well ☺

Cats also recognize different variations of their name and what it means when we use them. For instance, Nicky knows that when I am calling him by 'Nicky', or 'Nicky k'Nicky' play is probably coming, and that if I call 'Nicholas' he has done something wrong.

Now that we have looked at a couple of different ways cats associate names with individuals, as well as behaviors, we can look at another test. Call home sometime when you know someone will be there to answer the phone. Have that person put the phone on speaker phone and rerun the initial test from the beginning of this chapter (Saying names …). Note the kitty reactions.

Rating Opportunity: This is the time to test your cat's ability to understand human name association for themselves and those around the household. How did your kitty react on the test identified earlier? Did he respond when you called him by a different name? How about when you ask him where anther cat or a family member is?

- ❀ Give your cat 5 points for recognizing his own name as well as being able to recognize the names of other members of the household.
- ❀ Give your cat 3 points for recognizing his own name and no reaction to the unknown one used during the in person test.

Cat's Name	Category	Rating	Short Reason
Gabby	Name Recognition	+5	Gabby reacts to all names, her own and others. She also responds with recognition from the phone call
Nicky	Name Recognition	+3	Nicky reacts to his own name with ear twitches and turns to face the speaker. He has no reaction to any other names.

"I simply can't resist a cat, particularly a purring one. They are the cleanest, cunningest, and most intelligent things I know, outside of the girl you love, of course. "

Abroad with Mark Twain and Eugene Field, Fisher

Chapter 10: Purr-Ability:

Is there anything that can touch you more deeply in your soul than the adoring look and purr of your cat? They stare deep into your eyes with unconditional love and trust you implicitly. Just like human children, if you mean well and give love, you get massive amounts of love back. The purr of a cat looking at you is showing trust, adoration and contentment. This is a happy cat but happiness is not the only reason a cat will purr.

Cats purr for a number of reasons and sometimes they will purr at unlikely times. A purr can mean, "I am happy" or "Man, this spot in the sun is the best." Other purrs can be associated with pain or a plea to keep them safe. Let's tackle the most unusual one first, the purr to, "Keep me safe."

Purring at the Vet:

Nicky began to periodically get urinary tract crystals when he turned two. As you can imagine, this was a very scary time for both of us and we went to a number of vets attempting to resolve the issue. The vet visits required urinalysis, x-rays and the various poking and prodding that all doctors do. This is very scary for any kitty let alone one who doesn't feel well to start with. Nicky would purr throughout the entire visit as long as I was either holding him or stationed by his head. As soon as the vet would hold him, the purring would stop. I would step back in and it would begin again. The vets were all surprised and thought it was cute but we really know that Nicky was saying "Mom, please protect me." Some cats can also purr through pain. This wasn't the case with Nicky but it was the case in the next example with PM.

Purring Through Labor:

We already spoke a bit in the *Name Recognition* chapter about PM having her kittens. She purred from beginning to end. Now this purring may have had an association to the pain of birthing kittens but may also have had a benefit of helping her relax to make the queening easier. I think she was excited to see the little munchkins and probably also happy to stop carrying around the extended wriggling belly.

Purr-Love:

My favorite purr is the one emitted when your cat crawls on your lap for some one-on-one love and attention. How incredibly precious it is when kitty peers up at you with a look of utter adoration, eyes partially closed, as the most wonderful purring pours over you? You'd have to be made of stone not to melt right then and there.

Every cat purrs at different frequencies and volumes. Some purr low and slow, like a motor boat far in the distance that you can barely hear but can feel the vibrations against your hand. Some purr so loud you can hear them in the next room. A few of my cats would get so excited during petting that their purrs would get interrupted by periodic catches in their throat. Usually this happens while they are looking at the owner and in little kitty nirvana. Who says that cats can't show love?

Falcor was one weird little kitty. He was raised in our home by his mom PM (my cat) and his dad Tokar (my husband's cat). Out of all of PM's kittens, Falcor was the only one who preferred staying close to his mom rather than exploring with his brothers and sisters. He was always less comfortable around people and I think he thought we were ugly. I could just imagine he would look at me and wonder what horrible thing happened to my face that made me lose all my fur. And I wasn't the right color either! After all, his mother was all gray and all the brothers, sisters and father were white. On top of that, I was huge!

Over the years I think Falcor came to understand that humans and cats shared a home and helped each other. He slept with us and he had to be next to one of us on the couch or he followed me from room to room.

Falcor loved to lie in my lap and get massaged and petted. I would start with slow petting on the top of his head and over time move to stroking him below the ears and under the chin. After a couple of minutes of that I would return to the top of his head and start to apply a firmer touch while following the curve of his neck and shoulders. All the while Falcor would be purring deeper and louder with each pass. He would start to hiccup between strokes as he got more into it. Eventually he would forget himself and look up at my face to thank me. At that moment, all the memories or bad dreams about the human monsters would return. He would see my face smiling down at him, a look of utter horror would appear on his face and he'd run quickly out of the room. Falcor lived to twenty years of age with us and always had the same reaction to human faces. Most cats are the exact opposite of Falcor and seem to love the human face. Nicky loves to lie down next to me in bed and just stares at me while I pet him to sleep.

Gabby is also unusual in how she likes to be pet. I call it 'Baby Gabby.' Gabby crawls up into your arms, turns herself until she is spooning in your arms and stares up at your face. She likes to be pet in this position so she can look into your eyes. She only does the 'Baby Gabby' with specific family members. You have to be careful in the Baby Gabby position because Gabby likes to pet us back. She reaches out with her front paws to touch your face, lips or neck. She does have all her nails so it is a risky petting position.

The other risk in the 'Baby Gabby' is watching how deeply she gets into the petting. The more enjoyable she finds it, the more she wants to kiss you. Gabby's version of a kiss is a little nip. Now, it's not a bite - just a nip -

but it can still sting. She has successfully caught me on the chin a couple of time and the nose once. Ouch!

Sleeping Purr:

Purring is incredibly relaxing. When a cat crawls into my arms to spoon at night and starts to purr, no matter what my day has been like, I fall asleep within seconds. There is something about the rhythmic nature and vibration that just puts me out like a light. The only other things that affects me this way are the swaying of an overnight train ride and, for some reason, the take-off of an airplane.

Some kitties just come up and spoon while others have a process they need to go through before settling down. Nicky approaches as close to my head as possible avoiding other bodies, books or remotes then initiates the kneading phase. He extends and flexes each paw in his own rhythm until he is ready to cuddle up and spoon. Then the purring commences. He will actually purr without any contact from me but when I lean over to pet his chin and ears, the purring intensifies until you can hear him downstairs. At his point, Nicky likes to be cuddled almost like he is being swaddled. Hold him tight, if you are not cuddling tight enough, he will push back at you until you hug him closer.

Falcor on the other hand approaches the sleeping cuddle and purr differently. He approaches, sees a likely spot, moves everything else including bodies out of the way and literally flops down. The Falcor has landed. Let the purring begin. Just touch him anywhere and he purrs until he falls asleep. I can even read a book while just laying my hand on his side and he purrs away. Works for me too.

PM, being the prima donna she is, jumps up on the bed, sees a spot, moves everything out of her way and begins to knead... and then she kneads some more. She changes position, moves more stuff out of her way and kneads again. Changes her mind, sees a different spot, moves the items from the last spot back and kneads again. But no, this spot isn't right either, so she looks for another spot and starts kneading again until finally I say, "PM, find a damn spot." She moves to a new spot and finally lies down. Every single night, the same old song and dance but she is PM and there is no other like her.

Butterscotch likes to sleep at my head and chew on my hair, purring all the while. Now I know who to blame for the frizzies!

Gabby is totally different. She wants to cuddle and purr not when going to sleep but when waking up. Gabby sleeps at the foot of the bed but normally comes up to wake me up and get a quick cuddle and purr before the alarm goes off in the morning. Cool right? Nice way to wake up as long as she doesn't breathe on you.

Grooming Purr

Yes, we prefer to make grooming something the cats enjoy. I remember my mother brushing my hair as a child and how much I disliked it. I searched far and wide to find the appropriate grooming items to make my cats enjoy the process. Now this does not count trimming nails!

We'll cover grooming in detail in the next book about feline health and medical. For now, I can say that, as with toys, we have bought and tried everything. What my cats like is a simple, human comb. The kind used to cut hair. ☺ I start with the wide end to get kitty into the motions and within seconds he is holding his chin up so I can get to more real estate, purring all the while. If I find a knot, the thin side of the comb will untangle it as long as light passes are made that do not alarm kitty or pull the hair.

Purr-Avoidance

No, I don't mean that cats would ever avoid purring. Instead my cats have been known to use purring to avoid human contact when it is unwanted. At least, some of my girl cats do.

Have you ever approached a kitty and wanted to pet it but the cat was not interested? Butterscotch was a genius in this area. If she saw a person coming toward her when she had other things to do, she would attempt to swish out of the way. If, however, she was caught, she had plan B in her back pocket. She'd make pretend she was happy to be there and look like she was getting comfortable. The next step in her master plan was beginning to purr and to start pushing her head into your hands. As soon as you believed she was in kitty heaven, wham! She was "outa-a -there".

Rating Opportunity: Once again, I am going to equate the feline ability to modify and control his environment with an intelligence rating. Cats know that humans love their purring and do use that to modify our actions. Do you remember the last time your loved one gave you a massage? If you didn't verbally acknowledge that the caress felt fantastic, it would stop or be changed... just as it was feeling heavenly. Cats learn the same thing. "UMMM that feels good!" makes the massager keep it up.

What types of activities make your kitty purr? How does your kitty like to be pet? Does he enjoy a massage? What is the favorite spot or is there one that results in a stretch and the offer of more area to pet? Does your kitty ever pet you?

* Give your kitty 3 points for purring over and above the standard lap petting.
* Give an additional 2 points if kitty pets you in return as it shows the ability to relate an experience to another.

Cat's Name	Category	Rating	Short Reason
Gabby	Purr-Ability	+3	Gabby can be a very sweet and loving cat, WHEN SHE WANTS TO BE. Otherwise, don't pet Gabby unless she requested it.
Nicky	Purr-Ability	+5	Nicky may be the biggest love bug I have ever had. Not only is he up for a pet or massage at any time but he will pet you back.

"Cats are connoisseurs of comfort. "

James Herriot

Chapter 11: Cat's Sleeping Patterns

While big cats in the wild and feral cats may be nocturnal, most domestic house cats tend to be crepuscular, meaning that activity patterns spike at dusk and dawn. This explains my cats anticipating my alarm clock but getting stumped by daylight savings time ☺

Cats tend to adapt to their families' sleeping patterns as a general rule, simply by the nature of our relationship. As kittens they may sleep less at night which is easy to understand; there is just so much to do. Can you count the number of times your new kitten has woken you up in the middle of the night? Sounds of planters falling off of windowsills, shampoo bottles clanging in the tub, trash cans falling over and, of course, the inevitable squeaks and sounds of frenzied high tailing it away from the mayhem that kitty just caused. Over time these midnight rampages reduce in length and destruction until at some point the kitten begins to adjust to our sleeping patterns. Not all of them do, though.

Alex Sleeps Through the Night

Alex, our first male Somali, was a real cuddler and would spoon into my side and fall asleep whenever I did. When I woke up in the morning, there he would be in the same position with his little paw touching my arm. Every night he would climb next to me and in the morning he would be there ready to purr, cuddle and then push me out of bed to go get food. You get the picture.

One night I woke up at 2am, looked around, and was surprised to see no Alex. I went back to sleep and in the morning there he was in his regular spot. Hmm, what is going on here?

I forced myself to wake again, in the middle of the night, the following couple of nights to check and found that Alex was gone each night. In the morning though, there he was in the same spot he was in when I fell to sleep. He was cheating on our sleeping time!

What a cool little kitty right? Let's look a little more closely at the genius Alex was displaying:

- Alex somehow knew the humans expected him to sleep with them.
- He patiently waited until others went to sleep.
- Whatever it was that occupied him late nights, he did it quietly.
- He knew what time to return to bed so he wasn't missed.
- He remembered the exact position he was in the night before and returned to it.

Even though, at first glance, this seemed like such a simple action on his part, it actually took a good deal of intelligence to pull it off for so many nights without getting discovered.

This morning I rolled over and found Nicky in his usual spot and asked, "What did you do last night?" Nicky cocked his head to the side which makes me wonder if he is questioning why I was asking or wondering how I knew.

Rating Opportunity: Do you know what kitty does while you sleep? Where does your cat sleep? Are there special places kitty likes to spoon; behind the knees, under your arm or on top of your head? Does kitty usually stay in one spot or move throughout the night? If you have two kitties, do they fight for a favorite spot in bed?

- 🐾 Give your kitty 5 points if he managed to outsmart you or shows great insight into your sleep patterns.
- 🐾 Give your kitty 3 points if he manages to synchronize his sleeping patterns to yours.

Cat's Name	Category	Rating	Short Reason
Gabby	Sleeping Patterns: All night	0	Gabby sleeps on her own blanket at the foot of the bed. Periodically she'll come up and say hello but sleep for Gabby is a personal experience.
Nicky	Sleeping Patterns: All night	3	Nicky comes to cuddle as soon as bed time is made known, usually by shutting off the TV and lights. He is usually in the same general area at morning but in different positions or sides of the bed.

Gabby Keeps Bankers' Hours

While most of us in the house are up by 6:30 am, or so, to start the work day, Gabby doesn't let any of the hustle and bustle disturb her in the least. She sleeps right through it. Gabby starts to make movements around 1:00 pm, by stretching, front, back and then sides. She sits down to a short wake up bath and then finally crawls out of bed around 1:30.

Most adult cats sleep on an average between 15 and 20 hours per day. This is the inverse of human sleep patterns. I usually get about six hours of sleep and honestly can't remember the last time I got eight or more.

By the time Gabby gets out of bed, Nicky has already eaten breakfast twice, a late morning snack, and the first lunch. Nicky was a Hobbit in a former life.

Sleeping with Grace

Consider a kitty poised so carefully on the edge of the couch. His head and elegant neck draped over the end of the cushion with head pointed towards the floor upside down. How many times have I seen my cat do this and wondered how comfortable that can possibly be? Within a few minutes he stretches and his side moves ever closer to the edge. I am getting nervous for kitty. A deep sigh with a yawn is followed by the flexing of the tail which moves up,up,up... You guessed it- kitty, meet floor.

One day, I saw Falcor fall off of the windowsill. He hit the floor, shaking his head and looking at up at the bad sill that let him down. The next day I went to the pet store and purchased one of those window boxes to give him more space to enjoy the sunshine. Didn't matter, he fell off of that, too.

Rating Opportunity: This category can add, or subtract points from the overall score. How does kitty sleep outside the bed? Is there a favorite spot in the sun? Does kitty usually keep or lose balance on the sleeping perch?

- ☻ Give your kitty 3 points for consistently maintaining its perch without falling off.
- ☻ Subtract 3 points if kitty is continually falling off of sleeping perches. This shows a lack of knowledge about his body and the environment.

Cat's Name	Category	Rating	Short Reason
Gabby	Sleeping Patterns Graceful	3	Gabby rarely falls off of couches, windows or other perches when sleeping. This is not the case when playing, however.
Nicky	Sleeping Patterns Graceful	-3	Nicky falls off of the couch during sleep more often than the average kitty.

"The smallest feline is a masterpiece."

Leonardo da Vinci

Chapter 12: Cats; Graceful & Elegant?

While grace and elegance, or let's say, being able to keep ones feet under them, does not seem to be part of an intelligence quotient, knowing your physical nature and how you navigate in daily travels is worth taking into account. We are considering the kitty ability to interact with its environment and know its capabilities to be integral parts of intelligence.

Cats give the impression that they are regal animals full of grace and elegance. The stance of sitting straight up with their tails wrapped around their paws is particularly appealing. Is this first impression indicative of how they go about their daily activities?

Yeah, I don't think so. Most cats have a regal beauty but calling it grace and elegance may be taking it a bit too far. More often than not, you can catch them stumbling over their own paws and, of course, they look up at you with the "I meant to do that," expression followed up with the inevitable, "Are you laughing at ME?" Well, if they are not graceful they are indeed arrogant.

Cats do have a unique way of being able to manipulate their bodies during a fall so as to land on their feet. It is a very cool trick because I can't even do that rolling off the bed. By the way, the kitties are unable to contain their mirth watching my human inability to land well. I caught both of them staring at me on the floor from over the edge of the bed cracking up laughing and mentally high fiving each other. If you are wondering why I fell off the bed, it is because through the night, the cats kept pushing me closer and closer to the edge waiting for the inevitable to happen.

Considering that I am more than ten times their weight, it's a very cool trick for these intelligent, devious, baby mattress hogs.

Speaking of cats and falling, lots of kitties have fallen out of windows, or off balconies and yet, even the ones that have previously fallen, if they survive, will still get up on that ledge and look at you with a "What?"

Hang In There Baby!

Years ago when we lived in the west village of Manhattan, we were gifted with baby PM. Maybe in one of these stories I'll expound on the acronym but for now, let's just stick with PM. Our apartment was a standard village 2 bedroom where the bedrooms are so small that the only way you can fit anything in it is to have loft beds. Under the bed would be your desk or clothing and you climb a short ladder to get into bed each night. PM used to love running up the ladder and then doing a walk along the railing. I always told her to be careful and she would shoot me the kitty middle finger and bounce back and forth with her tail waving in the air. What a lunatic.

As you might have already guessed, there came a time when PM lost her footing. It was the funniest thing I had ever seen. As her foot slipped, she starting falling backwards and reached out with her front paws to grab at the railing. There she was, holding on with only a couple of claws on each front paw with her back legs cycling in an attempt to get a better hold. Her eyes were wide open, as was her mouth.

Figure 29- Hanging ©inna astalehova/Shutterstock.com

I reached out to try and grab her and 'poof' she was gone.

I heard a small 'puff' from the ground and leaning over the balcony saw that she had landed in my laundry basket, safe with a completely shocked expression. I couldn't help it and burst out laughing so hard I thought I was going to fall, too. She looked up at me and, if looks could kill......

Needless to say, she punished me that night by sleeping in the living room. It was the first time I got to fully stretch out in my own bed since she had arrived.

Gabby, on the other hand, I have never seen fall down from a height but she does often 'fall up' the stairs. She is running so fast - a whirling dervish - that she misses a paw placement and face plants on a stair. Like any normal kitty, she first looks around to see if anyone noticed. If she doesn't see anyone looking, she stops and licks whichever paw it was where the boo-boo occurred. If however she catches you looking, she gives a look like, "I meant to do that", turns to the side with her tail straight up in the air and ascends the remainder of stairs like a queen, very regal. Then she goes under the bed to lick her boo-boo in peace.

119

Magic Takes a Bath

My favorite part of being an IT traveling consultant is the relaxing bubble bath I treat myself with upon returning home. The cats are always fascinated at the idea of water in the bathtub to begin with. As soon as a bath or shower is completed, they can't wait to jump in to explore and figure out what the reason was for all the noise and mist.

One day, after a particularly trying client, I was relaxing in the bath with full-on bubbles, wine and a book. Magic was hanging out on the bathroom mat giving herself her own version of a bath.

I reached for a sip of wine and some bubbles floated up in the air and caught Magic's attention. She slowly crept closer to investigate. One paw at a time, right front paw, left rear paw, right rear paw, left front paw. One paw came up on the tub ledge and her face appeared over the rim. I blew a few bubbles in her direction. She backed away but then quickly came back up. A sniff here and there until Magic decided there was no danger and she jumped up on the ledge.

I put my book down and told her that this was a really bad idea. Magic turned, gave me a look of utter disdain and then immediately disappeared as she fell sideways into the tub. She freaked out for a bit seeking purchase until she finally found my leg to latch onto and jumped out of the tub. She took off running though the doorway leaving a trail of bubbles and wet paw prints.

I let the water drain out of the tub, wiped up the blood stains and put some anti-bacterial spray on my clawed leg. Lesson learned.

Rating Opportunity: This category can add, or subtract points from the overall score.

Is your cat graceful or does she trip on her own feet? How does she react when caught in a misstep? Think about the times that you have seen your cat fall off of railings. What about the jump from point A to point B that is miscalculated, leaving kitty shaking its head in frustration?

- Give kitty 5 or 3 positive points for grace and technical movements.
- Subtract points for kitty lacking the intelligence to correctly calculate gaps, heights or where to put those pretty kitty paws.

Cat's Name	Category	Rating	Short Reason
Gabby	Grace & Elegance	+3	Gabby puts on a good show and does want to look queenly but periodically falls short.
Nicky	Grace & Elegance	-3	Nicky doesn't really try to be graceful. You can see this in his play, which is full-on lion.

Nicky Takes a Shower

It's a good thing we are measuring the cat's IQ and not the owner's because some lessons I do need to learn more than once. After some time had passed, I forgot the rule about keeping the bathroom door closed while bathing and started getting lackadaisical again.

I was taking a shower after having worked long hours in the yard and letting the hot water melt away the sore muscles. After a bit to relax, I poured some shampoo on my hair, and spent a good minute or two lathering and massaging my scalp. Then I started rinsing out the bubbles. Have you ever been in the shower with soap in your eyes and had a strange feeling that something wasn't right? That is exactly what happened to me. I felt as if someone was watching me and, although I knew it was probably nothing, I just had to slit open my right eye to take a peek. Something was there, but all I could see through the burning soap was a fuzzy shape in the corner. Frantically, I tipped my face back into the spray to get the soap out of my eyes while trying to keep a small slit open to see if something was moving. I finally got some of the soap off, rubbed a bit and reopened my eyes. There he was. Nicky was in the shower, sitting down and facing me. His eyes were tightly closed, his ears were pinned back and to the side as water sprayed all over him. I gasped and Nicky opened his eyes. We stared at each for a couple of seconds until I repeated a Terminator phrase, "Get out." Nicky needed no further direction and the last thing I saw was a wet tail flying over the tub lip. It turns out that I no longer have to keep the bathroom door shut since Nicky had finally satisfied his curiosity.

"When I am feeling low all I have to do is watch my cats and my courage returns."

Charles Bukowski

Chapter 13: Kitty Gets In But Can't Get Out!

We have all heard the stories of the kitty stuck in the tree but I have never personally seen this, which is a shame, because I would love to see Superman swoop out of the sky to come save my cat.

What is it about cats that make them want to get into tight spots they can't get out of? Kitties love to climb into tissue boxes, circle themselves into the bottom of round bowls and even try and wedge themselves under tight spaces like the oven. For clever little balls of fur, they sure do get themselves into trouble.

What I have seen my little brilliant kitties do, though, is enough to make me wonder what they were thinking. Nicky, who almost never eats people food, got himself into a jam that would have been hilarious if it hadn't been so serious. Actually, looking back on it, I have to laugh at my fuzz ball but at the time I was not sure he would survive the situation that his natural curiosity led him into.

What's in There?

I had found some lovely stem less wine glasses and bought them for dinner parties. I figured these would be less likely to fall over or meet with accidents as I have already lost too many of my good crystal set.

They worked great! No breakage and people really liked them. After one party, I was in the middle of cleaning up in the kitchen, putting food away, when I heard some strange noises coming from the den. I quickly made my way to the area to find a strange looking Nicky. There was something wrong with his face but from the doorway I couldn't make out what it was.

I approached as he started racing around in circles. Then, he began walking backwards and I could clearly see there was one of my prized stem less wine glass stuck on his head. I stopped and caught him, then turned him around so we were facing each other. Remember, Nicky is the kitty who purrs, even at the vet as long as he can see me. It worked, he chilled out. It took a couple of minutes to wiggle the glass off of his head with me asking the whole time, "What were you thinking of?", "Why would you put your head in a glass?" along with a couple of choice words.

Apparently, a guest had left one of the new stem less wine glasses on a side table and Nicky was trying to smell whatever was at the bottom of it when he got his head stuck in the glass.

When I finally got him free he looked very funny. The fur on his head was all standing up and forward. He looked like one of those show cats... except his eyes were wide open with shock. Now that he was safe, I felt the overwhelming anxiety start to fade and began to crack up laughing. I was already on the floor next to him so I just rolled over and let the laughter come so hard tears started falling. Nicky was pissed.

On the positive side, I have never seen him approach another glass since. I threw out the stem less ones that night, in any case.

What's under there?
Gabby, or Gabrielle as she likes to be called, is a very inquisitive kitty. A closed door is a challenge to her. A sliding closet door should always be opened and a bureau drawer holds treasures that must be discovered.

I have never seen a more dexterous cat. Gabby can use her paws to get into things that I never thought a cat could manage. She grabs toys straight out of the air by extending her arm and bending her knuckles in to close her paw. She can also bat balls back at you or retrieve and return

124

them to you for another throw. All in all, she is a pretty smart little kitty. On the other hand, her curiosity at time gets her into hot water. Once something has been closed to her prying eyes, she just has to get to the bottom of it.

We had moved into a new apartment in Philadelphia that had sliding closet doors. The cats had never seen those before and were a bit confused at how they opened and closed. Eventually Gabby figured it out and she took the lead in sliding them open when any other cat wanted to get in. Nicky or Alex couldn't seem to get accustomed to the sideways motion so they would ask Gabby and... Viola!

Eventually, I started finding the inevitable pulls and tears in my dresses and business suits. It's not as if the cats do this on purpose but while they are investigating the closet a trouser leg or belt would brush by their head or tail, which is, of course, a call to battle! So we had to find something to keep them from opening the closet doors.

Magnets worked great. We put them on both sides of the door which made the force needed to open them a little too much for the kitties.

Life was good for about a week and then' the incident' happened. I came into the bedroom to find Gabby looking at me, screaming, with her left front paw stuck under the bottom of the sliding door. Apparently, after multiple tries to open the door by sliding it, she decided that maybe she could force it open by pulling at the bottom.

She got her paw under the door and then twisted sideways to attempt to pull it towards her. The door wouldn't move so she kept pushing her paw further under and upwards. She couldn't get the door to move in either direction and then she couldn't pull her arm out either, which really ticked her off. I had no idea what to do. I couldn't open the door without hurting her, couldn't twist her arm the right way and she wasn't listening to my directions, just crying. She was staring straight into my eyes screaming "Fix this!" followed up with, "I'll never put my arm under a door again, I promise."

Finally, I pulled the door upwards, huffing and puffing. At the same time, Paul knocked on the door which scared Gabby who immediately twisted her arm back to the correct position, extracted it and ran under the bed. Gabby was fine, two licks and she was back to normal, ready to put her arm under the door again.

We removed the closet doors and put them in the shed for safe keeping. Unfortunately, the shed was not waterproof and we got hit with a big chunk of our deposit taken to replace the doors when we moved. Cha-ching, kitty wins again.

In case you are wondering, Gabby still sticks her arm under doors but we found the answer is to make a loud noise to get her to extract herself, otherwise we would have no doors in our house!

Rating Opportunity: This is the opportunity to balance your cat's score by subtracting points for those head shaking, awe inspiring though ill-advised actions. Think about all those hair brained ideas your cat has had. How many times have you had to rescue kitty from distressing situations?

- 🐾 Subtract 3 points if you have had to rescue kitty
- 🐾 Subtract 5 points if kitty doesn't learn from mistakes and repeats the ill-advised actions.

Cat's Name	Category	Rating	Short Reason
Gabby	I'm Stuck	-5	Gabby is a very bright cat but gets caught in the most ridiculous situations and repeats them.
Nicky	I'm Stuck	-3	Nicky learned from his mistake and I have never seen him so much as approach a glass again.

"In ancient times cats were worshipped as gods; they have not forgotten this."

Terry Pratchett

Chapter 14: Kitty Revenge

You're spending a lazy, rainy Sunday on the couch and Jaws is just starting on TV. You aren't really interested but, despite yourself, you start to watch. After the opening and beach scenes play you remember the first time you saw this movie and sit back to get comfortable. In another 10 minutes the highly anticipated music starts. Da-Dum Da-dum Da-dum Da-dum Da-dum Da-dum, da-da-dum…. and then the cat jumps in front of the TV! Has this ever happened to you? It is not a coincidence. Remember, it is all about the cat!

Cats remember everything. Anyone who has ever been on the receiving end of kitty revenge has been made aware of this. Even the earlier stories of kitty getting stuck and repeating the action, does not belie this fact. The cat well remembers the pain and discomfort, but believes he can achieve a different outcome this time. We humans do the same thing or, as we say, it's the classic definition of insanity.

Since kitty remembers who does what, when and where, sometimes kitty can take her sweet time in returning the favor and carefully plan out the revenge or as one kitty told me, "Its justice!"

The classic case you may be already aware of is the pooping somewhere other than the pail. For instance, my friend Joy's cat, named Precious, absolutely hated Joy's boyfriend. Every time the boyfriend would come over, Precious would poop in his shoes. I think this is a pretty strong statement and very easy to understand. Cats do have a sixth sense when it comes to people. If your cat doesn't like someone, you can take that to the bank. Joy's boyfriend didn't stay around long... just long enough to piss off kitty.

My grandmother had a cat that would also show dislike for someone by pooping on the bathroom carpet. The person that cat hated was me! To make matters more interesting, the cat, Marshmallow, was my furry granddaughter. Did you get that straight? My cat, Butterscotch, had a litter including a beautiful girl that was black outside with a white belly who I named Marshmallow. Thus, if I am Butterscotch's mom, then Marshmallow was my furry granddaughter. Now my grandmother wanted a kitten so I gave her Marshmallow.

In any case, Marshmallow was very jealous of me. When I wasn't there, she got all the attention but when I stayed overnight for a visit, my grandparents doted on me. That was too much for this little fuzz ball to take and she would immediately poop on the bathroom mat. My grandparents tried to move the bathroom mat to the tub... the cat found it. They put it away for my visit and, instead, she pooped on the carpet just outside of the bathroom. Eventually they learned to keep any old bath mat around just for my visits. As I would walk in the door my grandfather would shout, "Edith, did you put out the old mat?"

Note: A cat that poops outside of its pail is extremely rare and will have a reason. If it is not, as I have noted here, a behavioral response to a specific situation, it could have a medical reason. If in doubt, speak to your vet.

Make it Personal

Up to now we have touched on a standard way for kitties to show disdain for some person and how that becomes a behavior that can be anticipated and understood. PM took this to a whole new level.

If you remember PM from the earlier stories you'll know that she is a pretty smart kitty so you would expect any revenge or 'justice' from her to be the topping on the cake and, indeed, that is the subject of our next example of kitty revenge.

My brother, Paul, and I were living in a west village apartment while each of us was attending a separate university. Things were going well - no arguments or issues. My brother was busy with his college studies and playing pool while I was taking a full class load and doing undergrad research in chemistry. I don't think we even had time to fight.

I was in my room studying when Paul came home, said "Hi" and went to his room. All of a sudden a bellow came from Paul like I have never heard before and PM immediately ran up the ladder to the loft. It reminded me of the battle cries you see in movies. I ran to his room to see what happened and there he was. He had dropped his bags to the floor and was staring at his desk in horror. His face was bright red and I thought he was going to explode. I looked at his desk and there, on his sketch books, drawing board, pencils, paints and keyboard was a big puddle spreading and dripping all over the floor. I asked what had happened and he spat out "Your cat peed all over my desk!" I crept closer and sure enough, kitty pee. Paul screamed from behind me, "Where is that &$^%# cat" to which I replied, "What the $&*$^# did you do to her?"

I never heard another word about the incident. Paul knew well whatever it was he did but I bet he didn't expect the little gift PM planned for him in return.

Fair warning: Don't mess with the cat!

Rating Opportunity: Be honest, have you ever done anything or heard of another in the family doing something that forced kitty to mete out some justice? We all have at some point. Think about the kitty response and rate its impact in changing the dynamics of his environment.

For Marshmallow, I think the pooping was expected behavior and had no negative impact on her treatment. I would give her 3 points for clearly making herself heard.

PM was different because her activities made a change in how she was treated so she made an impact in her world. I would give her 5 points.

Cat's Name	Category	Rating	Short Reason
Gabby	Kitty Revenge	+3	Gabby takes out all her revenge on Nicky. If I don't play with her, she hits Nicky. If she doesn't get food on time, she hits him. Get the point? Do what Gabby wants or Nicky pays the price.
Nicky	Kitty Revenge	0	Nicky, I don't think, would be capable of planning let alone carrying out, revenge.

Open the Door Now!

This is a story about protection and revenge. Protection, for the times a cat is looking after the well-being of those under its safekeeping and revenge when someone intrudes in that area.

Let me set the stage of the incident. At the time, we were living in the lakeside apartment in Chicago. The layout was a little strange in that the front door opened directly to the bedroom. The hallway from the bedroom led to the bathroom, then the living room a kitchen and the back door. We only used the back door to enter and exit the apartment as did all of our neighbors.

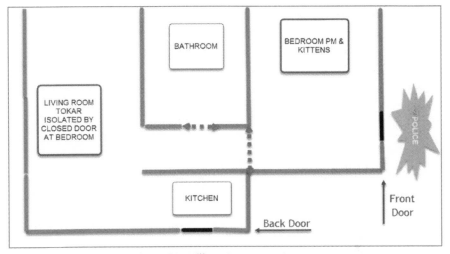

Figure 30 - Village Apartment Layout

PM had had her brood of six kittens two weeks earlier and we had to keep Tokar, the father, away from them. If PM saw Tokar anywhere near her kittens, she would chase him out of the house hissing and screaming the entire way. So Tokar was relegated to the living room and outside while PM and her kittens had the full run of the bedroom.

I had just returned home from work, checked in on PM and her kittens and fed PM. I was in the process of feeding Tokar in the kitchen when I heard a knock at the front door. I ignored it since that is not the common entrance our friends would use. Within a minute or two I heard another knock on the front door. I opened the drapes to see what was going on and was shocked to see at least 10 police cars with flashing lights out in the front. What the heck is going on? Again a knock on the front door and this time I can hear someone say, "Open the door now!" I put Tokar in the bathroom for a minute, ran through the bedroom, carefully closing the bedroom door behind me, and went to the front.

I opened the door to see about 8 police officers facing me with guns drawn. I put both my hands up and said something along the lines of 'Whoa, what's going on?" The policeman in the lead asked me quickly, "Are you firing a gun in here? Your upstairs neighbor is saying you are shooting through your ceiling." I was astounded. "Of course I am not shooting and I don't even have a gun." He asked to come in and check, which I agreed to. The other police in the hallway started to holster their weapons.

I let him in and quickly explained that we had a sensitive situation in the house due to the kittens arrival. I showed him PM and her kittens and we navigated through the closed door to the rest of the miniature apartment. He asked to see the bathroom, and opened the door. I caught Tokar when he bolted out the door as the police opened it. Satisfied that we weren't doing anything wrong, he gave me the okay and I put Tokar back in the bathroom until I got everything back to normal.

The police officer and I walked back to the bedroom where the other police were waiting. He smiled and said that he was sorry for the inconvenience and they all started leaving the apartment. As soon as the majority of officers left, PM decided that she had just put up with enough nonsense. She jumped into action by flying across the room and launching herself at the back thigh of the police officer. He screamed. I screamed. PM growled and the other police men spun around and pulled out their recently holstered guns. I put my hands back up and shouted "Cat! Just the cat!" The police officer was frozen still as PM continued to dig her claws into his leg and bite at his butt. I had to go over and extract her from his thigh one claw at a time while I knew he was holding back tears.

PM had a circle of protection in place for our bedroom. She wanted me to be there and put up with my husband but didn't want any other human or animals traipsing through. She saw a danger and did her best to retaliate. I can only imagine the story that police officer tells to this day. By the way, it turns out that my upstairs neighbor had stopped taking her Lithium a week before and had hallucinated the entire story.

Rating Opportunity: This rating opportunity is for reactive revenge rather than planned. Has your kitty ever been in the position to "educate a human" as a situational response? This sub-category will only add points to your kitty's score if deserved.

- Give your kitty 5 points if it has spontaneously jumped into action to protect loved ones.

Cat's Name	Category	Rating	Short Reason
Gabby	Kitty Revenge: Situational	0	Gabby has not had the opportunity yet.
Nicky	Kitty Revenge: Situational	0	Nicky has not had the opportunity yet.

"Women and cats will do as they please, and men and dogs should relax and get used to the idea."

Robert A. Heinlein

Chapter 15: Is your Cat Testing Your IQ?

Yes, kitty wants to know exactly how, when and why she can manipulate you. To a cat, she is quantifying your intelligence by her ability to push your buttons and get what she wants.

Cats rate us humans with their own scale of human intelligence. We fall into 4 distinct categories which are:

1. Bright: Almost cat-like
2. Average: Boring human but good playtime opponent
3. Dim bulb: Good at feeding but not much else
4. Silly human: Needs serious cat help to survive

Cats everywhere are testing their human family members and gaining an understanding of whom they can and cannot 'play' with. They know all of our idiosyncrasies better than we do. The standard cat can tell you who in the family is the one to ask for food or treats. Who the best play companion is or which lap is best for petting. Sometimes, this can be one member of the family but usually, they distribute their needs across multiple members. For instance, Gabby sleeps with me but is much more interested in playing with the men in the family. Gabby knows exactly which person she wants to request each activity from.

Perhaps your kitty does a little trick like PM does. PM looks so sweet and innocent when she is lounging on the floor in the hallway. I can't help myself but to stop and bend down to scratch by her ears, which always elicits a positive response with lots of purring. After a couple of seconds, when PM decides that she has had enough, a long stretch starts followed by a sudden shocked expression directed over my right shoulder. She is literally screaming silently, "Watch out Mom…. It's a monster!" As soon as I turn to look over my shoulder to see what was there, BAM she is gone. I could clearly hear her calling 'sucka' as she sashayed away tail waving in the air. In case you can't tell, I flunked this test which means I fall somewhere between dim bulb and silly on the cat's human mental acuity scale.

Once you are caught by kitty as less than the sharpest tack in the house, she will continue to test how often or which variations of the test you'll fall for.

Cats will also test your memory and know when the best time of day is to ask for certain items. For instance, Nicky will ask for food as soon as I walk through the door. It doesn't seem to matter how long I was gone either. I can wake up, feed Nicky, run out to the store to buy half and half for coffee and when I return, there is Nicky doing a good impression of a starving kitty wasting away for want of some kibble. I could tell him that he ate no more than 10 minutes before but that isn't the point. Nicky remembers when he ate; he just wants to test if I do.

Another memory test cats seem to do is expiration dates on items such as catnip toys. I must admit that I am starting to think that catnip smells pretty good. I think this is because I have to judge the strength of catnip toys before I buy them. If the catnip aroma is weak my kitties look at me and say, 'Seriously? Did you smell this? Stupid human!'

Rating Opportunity: This score is for you, not kitty. What would your kitty rate you as according to the kitty IQ scale for humans? Below are the example answers I think Gabby and Nicky would provide

Human's Name	Overall IQ Rating	Cat's name giving rating	Short Reason
Calla	3 – dim bulb	Gabby	This human is a dim bulb. I have to repeat myself over and over and she still gets it wrong!
Calla	1 – Bright, almost cat like	Nicky	Mom is the cat's meow ☺

"Time spent with cats is never wasted."

Sigmund Freud

Chapter 16: Putting It All Together and What Does It Mean:

I hope you had fun with the experiments and scoring kitty behavior to measure IQ. Using the rating table and categories may have had you reminiscing over past kitty mayhem with a smile. Please make sure to share your stories and ratings on the *Measure Your Cat's IQ* Facebook page at www.facebook.com/measureyourcatsiq

Now it's time to make sense of all the hard work you have done and scores you compiled. Gather the individual scores you have identified so far and let's collect them in a single rating table. You can use the blank template in the appendix or download the fully functional one from our Facebook page mentioned above, which will generate the averages and scales for you.

We'll look at the individual chapter test scores first and then calculate the overall IQ score. When this is completed you will be able to see which areas your kitty excels in and which ones could do with some more work.

Let's do the first one together.

Steps to calculate and understand the rating for the *Analytical Thinking* category.

There are four rating opportunities in this category. Retrieve your scoring sheet and look at only those tests that were included in the *Analytical Thinking* category we covered in the first chapter. Gabby's scores are added as an example in the table below.

1	2	3	4	5	6	7	8
Category	Devilish Genius	Psycho Superior	Average Kitty	Borderline Baby	Feeble Minded Fuzz Ball	Gabby's Score	Gabby's Category Rating
Out of sight test			0	-3	-5	0	
Pretend		3				3	
Cognitive Development	5					0	
Decision Making	5	3	0			3	
Sub-total	10	6	0	-3	-5	6	PS

Column numbers are added to the first table to make it easier to read and explain. The grayed out cells in a row mean you should not be able to score in this area. For instance, a Devilish Genius or Psycho Superior would have no score in the 'Out of site' test since these IQ levels would never be expected to fail this test. Only an Average, Borderline or Feeble Minded kitty could have any score for this particular test.

The columns contain the following information:

- Column 1: the name of the test in each category.
- Column 2: The potential score that a Devilish Genius would obtain
- Column 3: the score that a Psycho Superior would obtain.
- Column 4: The score that an Average Kitty would obtain.
- Column 5: The score that a Borderline Baby would obtain.

- Column 6: The score that a Feeble Minded Fuzz Ball would obtain.
- Column 7: A place to record your own kitty's test score. Gabby's scores are added in the tables throughout this chapter to use in examples.
- Column 8: The place to assign an IQ rating per category in the last row of the table called 'Sub-totals'. Gabby's ratings are added for examples to walk through.

Let's follow along with Gabby's results shown above.

1. For the 'Out of site' test, Gabby scored a 0 which aligns to the Average Kitty.
2. For the 'Pretend' test, Gabby scored a 3 which aligns with the Psycho Superior kitty.
3. For the 'Cognitive Development' test, Gabby scored a 0 which aligns with the score for an Average kitty.
4. For the 'Decision Making' test, Gabby scored a 3 which aligns with the Psycho Superior kitty.

The individual sub-total scores for each IQ level are; a Devilish Genius (DG) would score a total of 10 points, a Psycho Superior (PS) would score a total of 6 points, an Average Kitty (AK) would score 0 points, the Borderline Baby (BB) would score -3 points and the Feeble Minded Fuzz Ball (FM) would score -5 points.

The result is that Gabby's scores total up to be the same as the Psycho Superior kitty!

Now calculate the score for your kitty.

1. Place your kitty's score for each rating opportunity in the pink area (column 7). It should line up with one of the possible values in the white block.
2. Now, calculate the total score for your kitty on the last row.
3. Look at your kitty's subtotal and the subtotals for the 5 kitty IQ levels and choose the closest match to yours.

If you have our template from our website, this calculation will be automatically done for you.

So, how do we use this information? Analytical thinking is the ability to identify environmental factors and use logic to resolve issues or drive outcomes. Since you have gone through these tests, if your kitty scored higher than the average cat, you must be able to identify times or opportunities where you have noted this type of behavior. We can use this information to enhance our human-cat interactions as follows:

- If your kitty scored as a DG, then you are lucky to have a bright and adaptable cat that is capable of learning new things. Recommendation: continue to test your kitty with new ways it can expand its cognitive skills. Teach it tricks and look for toys that are more thought stimulating than simply chasing a bird on a wire. Kitty will love chasing the bird toy but also needs more advanced or challenging play activities that spark the mind. Tricks you can try to teach kitty are: jumping through hoops, finding specific toys or anything that will exercise kitty's mind.
- If your kitty scored as a PS, then this kitty should be getting more advanced types of play as well as the traditional kitty chase toys. Try teaching kitty simple tricks with a clicker and some treats such as following your finger or a pointer from spot to spot and learning new English words.
- If your kitty scored as an Average kitty, then you can also attempt to teach kitty some tricks as noted above but learning will take a longer time so patience is needed. But keep at it because exercising kitty body and kitty mind is good for all types of kitty IQ.
- If your kitty scored as a Borderline Baby, you may never get kitty to perform advanced tricks or play but speak to kitty often as you are working with him. For instance, while giving a kitty massage, rub its ears, saying "ear" and then point to your own. Even if kitty

is giving you a look like "Momma is nuts", it is hearing you and repetition will pay off in the end. Be aware of kitty's response though and don't frustrate him or yourself!

- And if your kitty scored as a Feeble Minded Fuzz Ball, then you have a real lover on your hands that will be happy with normal kitty play and tons of cuddling and lap loving. Periodically recheck your kitty's test and slowly start to add in some more advanced training if responses to stimuli become more advanced.

Now that we have gone into great depth in explaining the *Analytical Thinking* category, we can start to cover the results for each additional testing area in less detail. For the rest of the categories we will show the example rating table with overall scores and recommendations for each kitty IQ type.

Scoring for Verbal Communications Category:

Let's look at how chatty and effective your cat is.

Category	Devilish Genius	Psycho Superior	Average Kitty	Borderline Baby	Feeble Minded Fuzz Ball	Your Kitty Score	Your Kitty Category Scale
Human – Cat	5	3	0	-3	-5	5	
Super Hearing	5	3		-3	-5	5	
Singing	5	3		-3	-5	5	
Sub-total	15	9	0	-9	-15	15	DG

The highest achievable score for a DG is 15 but anything greater than 12 should be included as a DG. I would expect most kitties to score high points on the super hearing category. If your cat is deaf, please assign 0 points for this so it does not subtract from the overall score.

Regardless of your cat's score in this category, verbal communication in both directions is a tool you can build and increase over time. Keep your kitty journal up to date so you can learn new ways of understanding your cat over time. A template for this is in the appendix or can be downloaded from our Facebook page.

Here are the breakdowns for this rating opportunity:

- DG: If your cat is a verbal DG, you must have a great communication mechanism established with your cat. Recommendation: Keep speaking to kitty and attempt to establish new words in both English and kitty. Make a goal of teaching at least 3-5 new words per month. Some examples for consideration are: Chair, Bed, and Floor among others. Tie these into your play time.
- PS: the Psycho Superior kitty is capable of learning more ways to communicate verbally with you. Try to establish 1-3 new words per month.

- AK: The average kitty will learn new words over time dependent on the amount of effort you put in to training. Try to either learn 1 kitty word or teach 1 English word per month.
- BB: The borderline baby may have some trouble understanding English so it might be easier to deal with kitty by learning his spoken and body language skills.
- FM: the Feeble Minded kitty will follow along with the same recommendation shown above for BB. Remember you want to keep frustration levels low so it is vital to observer subtle body language.

Scoring for Non-Verbal Communications: How effective is Kitty at communicating through body language?

Category	Devilish Genius	Psycho Superior	Average Kitty	Borderline Baby	Feeble Minded Fuzz Ball	Your Kitty Score	Your Kitty Category Scale
Mirror Test	5	3		-3	-5	3	
The head tilt	5	3				0	
The blink test	5	3				5	
Kitty body expression	5	3			-5	5	
Sub-total	**20**	**12**	**0**	**-3**	**-10**	**13**	**PS**

The highest point score for non-verbal communication is 20 which indicate a very expressive kitty. The average kitty will still have ways of expressing with body language that may be more subtle and difficult to catch unless you are paying very close attention.

The most interesting recommendation in this category is that kitty will learn to 'express or not express' over time depending on our reactions. A kitty that does not get a response from repeated requests will tend to stop asking. We humans have the same reaction, don't we learn over time that throwing a tantrum will not get us the object of our desire? We learn to stifle the impulse and consider other ways of achieving the goal. Cats have a limited language to speak to us with so frustration and inability to communicate may make them stoical overtime. Our paying attention to kitty body language and attempting to understand kitty's intentions will eventually lead to kitty expressing more. Thus expect the ratings in this category to improve as you work with kitty. Now to recommendations:

- DG: If your kitty scored high in this category, much of the credit belongs to you as well. You are observing and responding to kitty so keep up the good work and see where you can improve.

- PS: You have built a great rapport with kitty but there are areas that can use improvement. Look at the individual test scores in this category to identify what is a good first step to work on.

- AK: Your kitty is speaking to you with good body expressions and you are paying some attention. You can certainly increase the scores in this category by keeping a journal and looking at those subtle signs that kitty is asking for assistance. You can help kitty make some great advances in this area if you choose to take on this challenge.

- BB: All kitties should be capable of at least scoring a BB in this category even with a total failure on the mirror test. Look back at your scores and try the test in this category again. Look very closely for the subtlest flicks of ears or whiskers. Try doing the test during play time when you know you have kitty's attention. As with the AK kitty recommendation above, this score can change overtime as you learn to identify the smallest body expressions. Expect these to get more obvious as you progress with kitty.

- FM: The Feeble Minded kitty may be operating under some serious deficiencies. Cats that are scared or nervous may stop expressing themselves through vocal or non-verbal communication patterns. Review your household and cat interactions to see if you can identify what if anything is the cause for this. A happy cat is comfortable in its surroundings and feels like a full member of the family. It might be funny to have a cat score as FM in this category but it is indicative of a deeper issue that needs to be resolved.

Scoring for Irrational Fear:

Some things are instinct that kitty has to learn to control, but we can assist.

Category	Devilish Genius	Psycho Superior	Average Kitty	Borderline Baby	Feeble Minded Fuzz Ball	Your Kitty Score	Your Kitty Category Scale
Vacuums	5	3				5	
Loud Noise	5	3				5	
Body Noises			0	-3	-5	-3	
Sub-total	10	6	0	-3	-5	7	PS

It can be funny, at times, when a loud noise scares the kitty but it can be indicative of a kitty who feels unable to understand and live confidently in the home environment. I also get scared or jump periodically when a car backfires or the fire alarm goes off at work, but I know there is a logical reason and quickly calm down. A cat may not be able to reason this out. There are some things we can do to lessen the impact. Let's look at some recommendations.

- DG: If your kitty scored a DG in this category, it is a very comfortable kitty that feels confident in the home and knows it is safe. Great job and continue the good work!
- PS: A PS kitty in this category feels mostly confident and safe but may have moments of terror. As with children, as much as we want to, it is impossible to protect kitty against everything. Look at what the causes are of kitty's fear and see what you can reduce or remove. Maybe it is time for that new vacuum? ☺
- AK: the average kitty will, of course, have moments of terror associated with loud noises. Some things that can help are to keep some comforting background noise so kitty isn't jumping at

every minor sound. Look at the fear factors to determine if there are any that can be removed from kitty's environment.

- BB and FM: I consolidated these two kitty IQ levels as the recommendation is very close for both. The most important area to evaluate is what is scaring kitty and look at ways to minimize the impact. If it is a matter of constant fear, we need to find a way to make kitty more comfortable and confident in the home. Try to increase the amount of play time and add in massage and kitty exercises. When loud noises do occur, try to calm kitty and explain that it will be okay. Cats respond to their owner's voice and a calm, quiet way of speaking will let kitty know that the world is not exploding. In extreme cases, swaddle your kitty. Cats are like infants in that they like to be swaddled and held tightly. A warm, comfortable but tight embrace along with calm reasoning and calling their name will alleviate the stress.

  Note* If kitty is uncomfortable in your embrace, try using a folded blanket to create a space that kitty can crawl inside.

One more item of note, I am a big proponent of the pheromone treatment. If your kitty seems to have fear above and beyond the average kitty in length or frequency, consider spraying the commonly used areas or purchasing the diffuser. This will remind kitty of the safety associated with their natural mother and should go a long way to relieving some causes of stress. I keep a bottle handy just in case kitty needs to make a vet visit.

Scoring for Play Expertise:

How did your cat rate at play?

Category	Devilish Genius	Psycho Superior	Average Kitty	Borderline Baby	Feeble Minded Fuzz Ball	Your Kitty Score	Your Kitty Category Scale
Type of play	5	3		-3	-5	5	
Kitty tricks	5	3	0			0	
Extra Credits	5	3	0			0	
Sub-total	**15**	**9**	**0**	**-3**	**-5**	**5**	**PS**

As explained in the chapter for play expertise, play time is extremely important to keep kitty's mind and body toned and balanced. It may seem like a small activity but the benefits of daily play can impact every area of your interaction with kitty including sleeping, eating and communications. Let's look at some recommendations for each specific IQ level.

- DG: If your kitty scored a DG in this category, congratulations, you are a wonderful kitty parent. This doesn't mean you can rest on your laurels though. To keep up the good work you should look at expanding the tricks and type of play. Set a goal to teach 2 new tricks a month and look for toys that provide choices for kitty but don't forget the plain, old kitty need for laughing, chasing and jumping. If you have never tried playing tag with your cat, this could be a great game to bring in. Get your cat to chase you around the house and then midway, start to chase kitty in return. Keep it non-threatening but a little jumping out at corners and then running the opposite way should get kitty chasing you in return. Watch kitty behavior to make sure it is enjoying tag as much as you are.
- PS: You and your kitty are doing very well to score a PS. You might have kitty performing some tricks and play often. Try and up the

game on the tricks by incorporating 1 new trick per month. Let us know how it goes. For ideas on tricks, check our Facebook page. Try playing the tag game listed above in the DG level.

- AK: The Average kitty should do well in this category. He has good play time experiences, may not be spectacular with tricks but is capable of learning more. Try getting a clicker and encouraging some new experiences for kitty to grow its repertoire in playing.

- BB: The Borderline Baby may have some trouble keeping up with more advanced play. This is okay. As long as kitty is healthy and happy, he can enjoy play and perhaps learn some new games. Try games that are a little slower. You can try the tag but instead of chasing you, use a toy on a string. Monitor kitty response and vary the speed and type of toy as needed to keep kitty interested.

- FM: All is not lost if your kitty is at the FM level of IQ for playing. Kitty will still be able to enjoy playing but may be much slower than the other levels. Read through the recommendations of the other levels to see if you can attempt to introduce more advanced types of play to your kitty over time.

Scoring for Boundaries:

Does your kitty respect your boundaries?

Category	Devilish Genius	Psycho Superior	Average Kitty	Borderline Baby	Feeble Minded Fuzz Ball	Your Kitty Score	Your Kitty Category Scale
Mine	5					5	
Yours	5	3		-3	-5	3	
Observations	5	3		-3	-5	0	
Respecting 'NO'	5	3		-3	-5	3	
Sub-total	20	9	0	-9	-15	11	**PS**

Boundaries are important for kitty safety as well as for us humans. We don't want kitty traipsing near the hot stove and certainly don't want to find kitty litter on the counter! Cats being what they are (smarter than the average human) only pay attention to boundaries because they want to please their pet parents. Let's look at some IQ specific recommendations.

- DG: The DG kitty rating is amazing. You have a kitty who respects your wishes because it loves and wants to keep you happy. Keep up the good work!
- PS: The PS kitty is doing very well but has some room for improvement. Look at how you are identifying the boundaries and how this is communicated. There may be some additional ways to enforce them such as explaining why the boundary is there for their own safety while redirecting kitty to another area.
- AK: The average kitty will pay attention to those boundaries kitty decides are reasonable. Sometimes kitty will challenge the boundaries to get attention. Just like a child, bad attention is better than no attention at all.
- BB and FM: I have consolidated these two levels as the recommendation is the same. As noted above, make sure your

kitty is not starved for attention. Choose the boundaries you want to enforce carefully. A limit of two to four boundaries are all you can expect. You have to explain to kitty why the boundary is there and then it is just a matter of vigilance. If you see kitty crossing a boundary, note the behavior that is preceding it so that the next time you can stop the breach before it happens. I am not a proponent of the electric mat and think that more can be accomplished with a calm, cool human head and vigilance.

Scoring for Hiding Objects:

Did you really think kitty didn't know? Silly human!

Category	Devilish Genius	Psycho Superior	Average Kitty	Borderline Baby	Feeble Minded Fuzz Ball	Your Kitty Score	Your Kitty Category Scale
Secret Stash	5	3		-3	-5	3	
Sub-total	5	3	0	-3	-5	3	PS

Of course, kitty knows where all the goodies are. Kitty doesn't even have to be in the room when you hide something and yet it knows where it is. Consider the example of buying a new pail, changing the location and putting all new sand down. Do you have to tell kitty where it is? No, kitty will find it. When wanting to hide things from kitty such as catnip, treats or anything that needs to be controlled, we have to decide what the most effective hiding place is. We know that cats can open cupboards, drawers, closets and even freezers. They can also get into cardboard, plastic bags or Tupperware containers. The recommendation for all kitty levels is the following:

- Keep toys, treats or anything else you want to hide from kitty away from the boundary areas.
- Use a cupboard that has a child safety latch on it.
- Don't hide it from kitty. That makes it a challenge any respectable cat will have to conquer. Let kitty know where it is and to come to you for distribution. Make them communicate!

Scoring for Eating Patterns and Food Cravings:

Kitty ate what?

Category	Devilish Genius	Psycho Superior	Average Kitty	Borderline Baby	Feeble Minded Fuzz Ball	Your Kitty Score	Your Kitty Category Scale
Food Caching	5	3	0			0	
Eating Patterns	5	3		-3	-5	-3	
Cuisine	5	3				5	
Sub-total	15	9	0	-3	-5	2	PS

There are some foods that are not good or even dangerous for cats. You can check a number of sites that will keep an updated list of food items to avoid. If you need help in your search, email me or check the Facebook page for this book. Here are some foods to avoid:

- Coffee, tea or alcohol (Yes, I know some dog people say they give their dog beer, but considering that cats are already smarter than the average human and ready to conquer the world, I would recommend leaving alcohol off the kitty diet!)
- Onion and garlic
- Chocolate
- Grapes and raisins
- Raw meat

Having said this, it is pretty common to find a cat owner who gives the occasional kitty treat from their own plate. Remember that prepackaged kitty food, at least the good ones, have added protein and nutrients that are necessary for the health of kitty.

[Please see your veterinarian if you have any questions.]

Calla H Knopman

Scoring for Name Recognition:

You called me what?

Category	Devilish Genius	Psycho Superior	Average Kitty	Borderline Baby	Feeble Minded Fuzz Ball	Your Kitty Score	Your Kitty Category Scale
Name	5	3				5	
Sub-total	5	3	0	0	0	5	DG

I only put in acceptable values for DG and PS in this category. I have not yet seen a cat that does not recognize his own name. If you disagree, please send me a note so I can adjust for other readers.

- DG: The DG kitty should get credit for knowing multiple names for themselves and the other household animals or people. This is one really smart kitty.
- PS: The PS kitty knows his name but may not react during the test to the calling of other names. This could be either that kitty is simply not incented to know this information or knows it but is practicing selective hearing. Try the test again but this time offer a treat when kitty readily identifies the person you call. Does that change the score? I thought so ☺

154

Scoring for Purr-Ability:

You like that kitty?

Category	Devilish Genius	Psycho Superior	Average Kitty	Borderline Baby	Feeble Minded Fuzz Ball	Your Kitty Score	Your Kitty Category Scale
Purr-Ability	5	3				3	
Sub-total	5	3	0	0	0	3	PS

All cats, with some small exceptions, can purr. There may be different types of purrs or variations on frequency, tone or vibrato but the general house cat will purr. An exception to this would be an anatomical reason such as an issue with vocal chords. Some cats may purr so low that it is difficult for humans to detect it. If you think your cat is not purring then follow this test: Pet them where you know they like the feeling. If you can't hear any purring, lightly place your hand under kitty's chin to be able to detect any vibrations in the throat. Do you feel any vibration?

- DG: The DG cat not only recognizes its own pleasure but wants to make sure you feel it too! This cat, by petting in return is showing empathy.
- PS: The PS kitty purrs to show trust and faith in you. This kitty may not grow to be able to pet you back but you might find it interesting to repeat this test after following some of the other recommendations on playing and tricks.

If you have a new rescue kitty or are turning a feral cat into a pet, you may have trouble getting the purr until they have warmed up to you and feel safe and secure. Follow the recommendations in the *Fear* section, consider pheromones and most of all practice patience! The rewards that will come later are well worth the effort.

Scoring for Sleeping Patterns:

That position is comfortable?

Category	Devilish Genius	Psycho Superior	Average Kitty	Borderline Baby	Feeble Minded Fuzz Ball	Your Kitty Score	Your Kitty Category Scale
All night	5	3	0			0	
Graceful	5	3	0	-3	-5	3	
Sub-total	10	6	0	-3	-5	3	PS

There were two distinct aspects we covered in the *Sleeping Patterns* chapter, cats' behaviors during human sleep time, and cats' abilities to balance and keep their positions during kitty sleep.

- DG: If your cat scored a DG in this category, then kitty is smart enough to know that a human parent who does not get enough sleep is no fun to be around and kitty is also graceful enough to keep his perch when snoozing. This is an ideal rating.

- PS: The PS score indicates that kitty may be not so graceful when asleep and rolls off the surface of the chosen nap area. This may not be that different than for humans. Let me add here that rolling off the bed is not one of the criteria used in calculating human IQ so we should not really include it here but an awareness of the body for a cat is very important as we will see with the next scoring section.

- AK, BB and FM: Let's tackle the first issue about kitty up playing while the humans are sleeping. If this is robbing you of necessary sleep time, then move your playtime closer to the time you generally retire for the night to let kitty expend it's energy and be ready for rest. Start getting kitty in the habit of eat, then play, then sleep, and you may get better rest at night. The second issue on of falling off sleeping beds, couches, or other unique kitty perches, will be covered below.

Scoring for Grace and Elegance:

Kitty fell off what?

Category	Devilish Genius	Psycho Superior	Average Kitty	Borderline Baby	Feeble Minded Fuzz Ball	Your Kitty Score	Your Kitty Category Scale
Grace & Elegance	5	3		-3	-5	3	
Sub-total	5	3	0	-3	-5	3	**PS**

Yes, our regal little kitty may not look quite so royal when leaping nowhere, falling off railings or sliding on its butt. Let's look at this in two distinct paths: kitty is falling because it is trying something new and challenging or kitty is falling because he is not aware of foot placement and surface sturdiness.

Firstly, cats are very curious creatures so they may find a challenge that they cannot resist. Unfortunately, some of these challenges may leave kitty looking a bit put out when things don't work out as planned. We spoke in the *Graceful & Elegant* chapter of cats balancing on rails and bathtub rims neither of which provided a surprise to the human when they fell off. Part of the reason for the 'fall from grace' is the arrogance of kitty. As a matter of fact, if the cat wasn't so busy prancing around, it might not have fallen.

For this reason, I am going to make a judgment call that most of the errors in grace happen to kitties in the DG and PS range. A kitty with a lower IQ will tend to take more time and worry about the placement of the feet, thereby falling less often.

- The recommendation for all cat IQ levels is to improve the agility of kitty via training. You can make this one of the tricks you want to work on as your goal.
- Have kitty walk along a long slim board (close to the ground of course).

- Have kitty leap from place to place, increasing the space between so that kitty gets to be a better judge of distance and physical capabilities.

Scoring for Cat gets stuck:

You climbed in what?

Category	Devilish Genius	Psycho Superior	Average Kitty	Borderline Baby	Feeble Minded Fuzz Ball	Your Kitty Score	Your Kitty Category Scale
I'm Stuck			0	-3	-5	-5	
Sub-total	0	0	0	-3	-5	-5	FM

Please don't think I am cruel but I can't help but crack up sometimes seeing what my cats have thought up to try. It is only the times where I question their safety that I get concerned.

- AK: The average kitty will get stuck in certain situations at one time or another but this kitty will learn from the error and tend to not repeat it. There is nothing we can really do to completely protect a cat against its own kitty curiosity but we do our best to kitty-proof the house.
- BB: The Borderline Baby may indeed repeat a process that had already proven to be a bad idea. For this kitty, we need to observe and notice when these events happen and take the time to lecture kitty about safety.
- FM: The Feeble Minded kitty may be doomed to repeat a failure without learning from it. For these kitties it is imperative to remove the cause of the issue. For instance, I gave away the stem-less wine glasses as it wasn't worth the risk.

Scoring for Kitty Revenge:

A dish best served cold?

Category	Devilish Genius	Psycho Superior	Average Kitty	Borderline Baby	Feeble Minded Fuzz Ball	Your Kitty Score	Your Kitty Category Scale
Kitty Revenge	5	3	0	-3	-5	3	
Sub-total	5	3	0	-3	-5	3	PS

Yes, my kitties watch Star Trek and love this line. I am always astounded at folks who say cats can't think or don't remember from one moment to the next when it is crystal clear they are wrong.

Now, there really is no recommendation that can be given for this section other than common sense. It doesn't matter if the cat is a Devilish Genius or a Borderline Baby, a cat that has been ill-used will find a way to return the favor.

Recommendation: Treat kitty as you would want to be treated.

The Overall IQ Rating

Now that we have been through all the individual scores, let's tabulate the grand total and check it against the scale. The classical method to illustrate IQ ratings is a bell curve. The majority of cats, roughly 50% will fall within the Average Kitty rating. The two neighboring ratings for Borderline Baby and Psycho Superior will include approximately 30% percent of the cats. The remaining cat population will be rated in the Feeble Minded Fuzz Ball or Devilish Genius groups.

To see where your kitty IQ level is, calculate your grand total from the rating table and compare that against the ranges below.

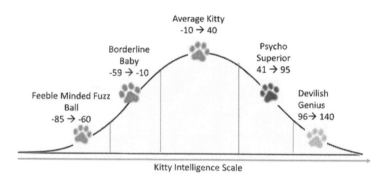

The range of values are shown in the bell curve above or detailed in the list below:

- Devilish Genius scores between 96 and 140.
- Psycho Superior scores between 41 and 95.
- Average Kitty scores between -10 and 40.
- Borderline Baby scores between -59 and -11.
- Feeble Minded Fuzz Ball scores between -85 and -60.

These scores have no impact on my love for them but does give me direction on what needs I should look to satisfy for each cat. For instance, Gabby scored a 74 which rates her as a Psycho Superior. Gabby is a very inquisitive kitty which comes out in her test scores. She needs to be kept challenged to keep her brain active and involved. She scored highest on *Name Recognition* & *Verbal Communication* so I am going to extend her training in those areas by adding new people and object names and rewarding positive behavior. Gabby scored the lowest in *Kitty Gets Stuck* because she cannot resist the call of a closed door. For this issue, I have installed guards on the bottom of the doors to prohibit little kitty paws from getting stuck and am working on training for which doors can be opened. Fingers crossed!

Nicky scored a 31 which rates him as an Average Kitty though he scored much better in playing and tricks. I am dedicating more time to training to help him achieve new goals to feel good about. Nicky scored lowest on *Grace & Elegance* and failed the *Kitty Gets Stuck* category. This requires a two-pronged approach. First, the tricks Nicky already does need to be extended to teach body size and capabilities such as walking along a very thin board. Second, retesting for getting stuck in the stem less glass. Nicky has never gotten stuck in anything since the 'incident' so it is time to retest and remove the failing score if he has learned where not to stick his head ☺

Now, to your scores. You have calculated both the individual and for overall IQ scores. Look back at your kitty's category specific scores and see which areas you can use to strengthen your bond with kitty. This is also a great way to bring other members of your family into the interaction. For instance, if you have a younger child or significant other who doesn't like or trust kitty, have them help you with the testing or follow up training. Getting a glimpse into the kitty mind is to fall in love with the kitty.

All felines need love and patience. From the Devilish Genius to the Feeble Minded Fuzz Ball, cats will have moments of brilliance and moments of idiocy. For a fuller more satisfying relationship, find your cat's strengths and play to them. This will make your cat more confident and self-assured of its place in the home. Happy cat, happy family!

Acknowledgements

Thank you to my family, both human and fur balls who put up with and supported me in this endeavor; Martin, Phyllis, Harry, Ron, Pam, Jacob, Gabby, & Nicky.

Thank you to my extended family and Shabbat aficionados who shared with me their stories, reviews, and the love of our pets and each other: Elliott, Jay, Vivian & Gabe, Kathleen & Ron, Elaine, Sally & Bernie and others.

Thanks to my reviewers as this is my first book, I appreciate your time and patience. You guys are great! Martin, Janie and Janet.

Finally, thanks to all the kitties that have made my life so enjoyable and given me so much material that many stories got left out of this book.

Appendix:

IQ Score Summarization Table:

The table below can be utilized to sum your kitty's IQ scores for each category as well as the total overall IQ. Each category is broken down by chapter and individual test. The white squares below indicate potential scores for each test. Place your kitty's test score in the last column to the right which are pink if you are viewing online.

Sum up all the pink boxes in the 'Your kitty Scores' column to get the total IQ score. Sum each subtotal in the orange rows to calculate the score per category.

Chapter	Category	Devilish Genius	Psycho Superior	Average Kitty	Borderline Baby	Feeble Minded Fuzz Ball	Your Kitty Score
Cats - Analytical Beings	Out of sight test			0	-3	-5	
	Pretend		3				
	Cognitive Development	5					
	Decision Making	5	3	0			
	Sub-total	**10**	**6**	**0**	**-3**	**-5**	
Verbal Communication	Human - Cat	5	3	0	-3	-5	
	Super Hearing	5	3		-3	-5	
	Singing	5	3		-3	-5	
	Sub-total	**15**	**9**	**0**	**-9**	**-15**	
Non-Verbal Communication	Mirror Test	5	3		-3	-5	
	The head tilt	5	3				
	The blink test	5	3				

	Kitty body expression	5	3				-5
	Sub-total	**20**	**12**	**0**	**-3**	**-10**	
Irrational Fear of Noise	Vacuums	5	3				
	Loud Noise	5	3				
	Body Noises			0	-3	-5	
	Sub-total	**10**	**6**	**0**	**-3**	**-5**	
Playing Expertise	Type of play	5	3		-3	-5	
	Kitty tricks	5	3	0			
	Extra Credits	5	3	0			
	Sub-total	**15**	**9**	**0**	**-3**	**-5**	
Boundaries	Mine	5					
	Yours	5	3		-3	-5	
	Observations	5	3		-3	-5	
	Respecting 'NO'	5	3		-3	-5	
	Sub-total	**20**	**9**	**0**	**-9**	**-15**	
Don't Bother Hiding That	Secret Stash	5	3		-3	-5	
	Sub-total	**5**	**3**	**0**	**-3**	**-5**	
Eating Patterns and Food Craving	Food Caching	5	3	0			
	Eating Patterns	5	3		-3	-5	
	Cuisine	5	3				
	Sub-total	**15**	**9**	**0**	**-3**	**-5**	
Name Recognition	Name	5	3				
	Sub-total	**5**	**3**	**0**	**0**	**0**	

Measure Your Cat's IQ

Purr-Ability	Purr-Ability	5	3			
	Sub-total	5	3	0	0	0
Sleeping Patterns	All night	5	3	0		
	Graceful	5	3	0	-3	-5
	Sub-total	10	6	0	-3	-5
Cats: Graceful & Elegant?	Grace & Elegance	5	3		-3	-5
	Sub-total	5	3	0	-3	-5
Kitty Gets In, But Can't Get Out!	Kitty Gets in: I'm Stuck			0	-3	-5
	Sub-total	0	0	0	-3	-5
Kitty Revenge	Kitty Revenge	5	3	0	-3	-5
	Sub-total	5	3	0	-3	-5

Cat Communication Journal:

Use the journal below to start building your own kitty vocabulary. Incorporate whatever spelling or pronunciation techniques will help you recall the vocalization so you can learn it.

Note the time, reason or other non-verbal expressions that will help to indicate kitty's request. Have fun!

Day	Time	Sound	Reason	Body Motion	Can you imitate

About the Author

Calla Knopman is the proud parent of perhaps the world's smartest and long lived felines. Her relationship with her cats evolved from a life-long love of kitty characteristics and nature. Calla works as an IT consultant to support her cats in the lifestyle they have become accustomed to. They all live happily in suburban Philadelphia.

Calla can be reached at MeasureYourCatsIQ@gmail.com

Figure 31-Me as a 'kitten' on my first day of school. Not sharing the date.

Made in the USA
Columbia, SC
12 March 2019